The Great Siege of Chester

The Great Siege of Chester

John Barratt

TEMPUS

First published 2003

PUBLISHED IN THE UNITED KINGDOM BY:
Tempus Publishing Ltd
The Mill, Brimscombe Port
Stroud, Gloucestershire GL5 2QG

PUBLISHED IN THE UNITED STATES OF AMERICA BY:
Tempus Publishing Inc.
2 Cumberland Street
Charleston, SC 29401

British Library Cataloguing in Publication Data.
A catalogue record for this book is available from the British Library.

ISBN 0 7524 2345 2

Typesetting and origination by Tempus Publishing.
PRINTED AND BOUND IN GREAT BRITAIN.

CONTENTS

ILLUSTRATION LIST

Illustrations courtesy of John Barratt unless otherwise stated.

Chronology

1639

First Bishops' War.

1640

Second Bishops' War.

18 September   Order for repairs to Chester defences. Francis Gamull made captain of city Trained Band.

1641

October   Outbreak of rebellion in Ireland.

1642

4 January   King fails in attempt to arrest five leading opponents in Parliament. Civil War becomes inevitable.

8 August   Sir William Brereton expelled from Chester after attempting to recruit for Parliament.

22 August   King raises standard at Nottingham. Official start of Civil War.

6 September   Chester assembly orders further repairs to defences.

23–28 September   King Charles I in Chester, secures election of pro-Royalist William Ince as mayor.

23 October   Battle of Edgehill; marginal Royalist victory.

1643

3 February	Order by Chester assembly for levying of £500 for construction of outworks to protect suburbs.
13 March	Cheshire Royalists defeated at Middlewich. Sir Nicholas Byron appointed governor of Chester.
18–21 July	First attack on Chester by Sir William Brereton repulsed.
16 September	Cessation signed between King and Irish Confederates.
7 November	Brereton takes Holt Bridge then occupies north-east Wales. Lord John Byron appointed 'Field Marshal General of North Wales and those Parts'.
21 November	English troops from Ireland land at Mostyn. Brereton retreats across Dee.
4 December	Hawarden Castle surrenders to Royalists.
12 December	Byron begins Nantwich campaign.
13 December	Royalists surprise Beeston Castle.
24 December	Bartholmley 'Massacre'.
26 December	Royalists defeat Brereton at Middlewich.

1644

6 January	Prince Rupert appointed captain-general of Wales and the Marches.
18 January	Royalist assault on Nantwich repulsed
25 January	Battle of Nantwich: Fairfax defeats Byron.
11 March	Prince Rupert visits Chester and orders alterations to defences. Gamull fails in bid to become governor.
18 May	Rupert and Byron begin Lancashire campaign.
19 May	William Legge appointed governor of Chester.
11 June	Rupert takes Liverpool.
2 July	Royalists defeated at battle of Marston Moor.
21 August	Colonel John Marrow defeated and mortally wounded at Tarvin.
18 September	Byron defeated at Montgomery.
October	Brereton begins to close in around Chester.
1 November	Parliamentarians take Liverpool.
December	Leaguer of Chester begins.

1645

18 January	Royalist defeat at Chrisleton.
January/February	Lord Byron becomes governor of Chester.
19 February	Prince Maurice relieves Chester.
22 February	Parliamentarians surprise Shrewsbury.
13 March	Maurice leaves Chester. Siege resumed.
15 March	Rupert and Maurice relieve Chester and Beeston.
16 May	Leaguer again raised by Brereton on approach of Royalist 'Oxford Army'.
14 June	'Oxford Army' defeated at Naseby.
28 July	Leaguer of Beeston Castle resumed.
20 September	Parliamentarians surprise Chester suburbs.
22 September	First Parliamentarian assault on city repulsed.
23 September	King Charles enters Chester.
24 September	Royalists defeated at battle of Rowton Heath.
25 September	King Charles leaves Chester.
9 October	Second major Parliamentarian assault on city repulsed.
1 November	Battle of Denbigh Green. Sir William Vaughan's relief attempt defeated.
10 November	Parliamentarians begin mortar bombardment of Chester.
25 November	Last major Royalist sally repulsed.
10 December	Major damage from Parliamentarian mortar bombardment.

1646

7 January	Brereton summons to Chester to surrender rejected.
14 January	Byron orders survey of food stocks in Chester. Increasing protests among citizens.
29 January	Surrender negotiations begin.
30 January	Surrender terms agreed.
3 February	Chester surrenders.

INTRODUCTION

In most accounts of the English Civil War, the spotlight falls on the great set-piece battles such as Edgehill, Marston Moor, Naseby and Worcester. This is both understandable and justified, for such dramatic actions could change the course of events in a few hours of bloody combat. Yet equally significant in its ultimate effect was the 'other' war of countless skirmishes and scores of sieges, ranging across virtually the whole of the British Isles in the decade following 1641. The outcome of these often little-known episodes would eventually decide the control of vast tracts of the country, possession of which was vital for the war efforts of the opposing sides.

Although marauding armies might leave a swathe of looting and wanton destruction in their path, the major battles rarely had any direct impact on the civilian population other than the conscripts enrolled in the opposing armies, the unfortunate camp followers caught up in the action and farmers unlucky enough to have their fields turned into battlegrounds. Sieges, however, especially those of towns and cities, involved all of their inhabitants – men, women and children of all classes and backgrounds – bringing them direct and sometimes prolonged experience of all the manifold dangers and horrors of war.

Chester was one such place. Prosperous, and perhaps a little complacent, on the outbreak of war in 1642 its citizens had the misfortune to be living in a location of prime strategic importance to both King and Parliament. The result, as Chester became a pawn on the chessboard of war, were three years of constant threat, alarms and upheaval, culminating in one of the longest sieges of the Civil War, which reduced much of Chester to ruins and left its starving population ripe for the ravages of plague.

A wide range of contemporary sources, including the journal kept during the siege by a Chester alderman, the detailed account of the final months of the siege written by the Royalist governor, the letters of the Cheshire Parliamentarian commander and extensive civic and personal records provide a vivid and comprehensive portrait of the impact of the Civil War on Chester, its people and the soldiers involved on both sides.

This is the first detailed account of one of the key sieges of the English Civil War to appear in the last eighty years, and makes use of a number of sources and much research which have appeared in the intervening period, adding greatly to our knowledge of many aspects of the Civil Wars.

Thanks are due to the patient and knowledgeable staff of a number of libraries and institutions, notably Chester Record Office, Cheshire County Record Office, Chester Public Library, the Sydney Jones Library, University of Liverpool, the British and Bodleian Libraries, the Grosvenor Museum Chester and Chester Heritage Centre. Numerous individuals have also provided invaluable information and insights whilst I was researching this book. They include Ivor Carr, John Lewis, Les Prince, Stuart Reid, Keith Roberts, David Ryan, John Tincey, Simon Ward and the late Norman Dore.

Thanks are also due to Stephen Beck and Derek Stone for the line drawings and maps.

Chester remains a city steeped in its history, and not even a casual visitor, still less one with an interest in the Civil Wars, can walk its streets and walls without constant reminders of Chester's role in this turbulent episode of British history. Awareness of this, and of the men, women and children, of all sorts and conditions, caught up in these events, have been with me throughout researching and writing this book, and if the end result conveys some inkling of this to those who read it I will be well satisfied.

John Barratt
September 2002

I

'MOST ANCIENTE CITIE': CHESTER IN 1642

In 1612, when the cartographer and historian John Speed published his great atlas, *The Treatise of the Empire of Great Britain*, the plate depicting his native county of Cheshire included, in pride of place, a plan of 'that most ancienté citie' of Chester.

From Roman times, Chester had played a leading role in the life of its region and the country as a whole. The town was of great geographical and strategic significance. It was situated on a low hill to the east of the River Dee, with other rising ground on the west bank of the river. The gullies which ran down either bank formed the lowest bridging point of the Dee.

Chester was the gateway to North Wales. Its bridge was not the only point at which the lower Dee could be crossed, for downstream there were fords over the estuary, shifting and treacherous traps for the unwary, at Blacon and Shotwick, and upstream, 6 miles south of Chester, another bridge at Farndon. But the main route to North Wales, whether for Roman legionaries, Norman earls, Plantagenet kings, and merchants and traders of all times, had always run through Chester. Chester also dominated the western route to Scotland through Cheshire and Lancashire via the crossings of the River Mersey at Hale Ford and Warrington.

For centuries Chester had been a considerable port. Its ships could be seen in harbours all around the British coast, and its seamen and merchants were encountered as far afield as France, Portugal and Spain. Most important, however, were the city's links with Ireland. Its ships carried the trade of the Irish Sea, and, in time of war, English armies and their supplies. As recently as

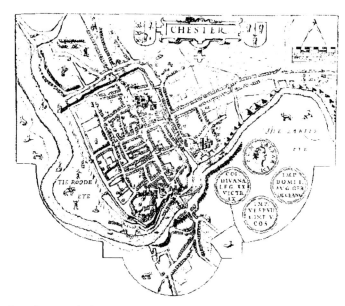

1. John Speed's map of Chester, 1610. Note that the River Dee ran much closer to the western wall of the city than today. Significant suburban development had occurred to the north and east of the old city, and at Handbridge on the southern bank of the Dee.

1641, when rebellion broke out in Ireland, Chester's streets and taverns had been filled with swaggering brawling soldiery on their way to the wars.[1]

But by the opening of the seventeenth century, the greatest days of the port of Chester lay in the past. The silting-up of the Dee Estuary had been a problem for over 200 years, and in the mid-sixteenth century the New Quay was built at Neston, nearer to the mouth of the river. This became the harbour for larger vessels, though smaller ships continued to make their way upstream as far as Chester itself. Neston was the main embarkation point for troops sent to Ireland. The importance of the city's links with Ireland would grow during the Civil War, when Chester and its port were the main landing places for English troops recalled from the province of Leinster to serve the Royalist cause.[2]

As Speed's map shows, early seventeenth-century Chester still had close links with the surrounding countryside. By 1642 the city's population totalled between 5,000 and 10,000. Numbers had been rising steadily since the previous century, despite temporary setbacks resulting from regular visitations of the plague, the most serious of which, in 1603–04, had killed 1,000 people.[3]

Chester remained a fairly compact city. The majority of its inhabitants lived within the circuit of its largely intact medieval city walls. Most of the principal

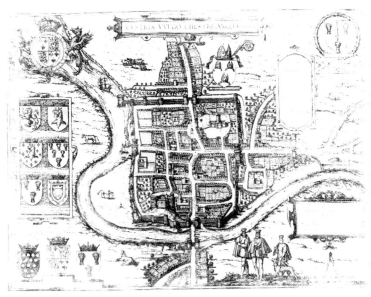

2. Braun and Hogenburg's map of Chester from *Civitates Orbis Terrarum* (1585). Note the shipping on the Dee, and the cross on the Roodeye (itself used for grazing livestock). The allotments and orchards in the western part of the city are clearly visible, as are the gardens behind many of the larger houses such as those on Eastgate and Bridge Streets.

buildings were situated along four main thoroughfares, Eastgate Street, Bridge Street, Watergate Street and Northgate Street, which followed the plan of the old Roman fortress. Here were the shops and dwellings known as the 'Rows', whose unusual construction excited much comment from visitors.[4] Dotted along the streets, among the churches, shops and taverns, were the richly ornate half-timbered homes of Chester's leading merchants and the town houses of the gentry of west Cheshire and north-east Wales. Behind these streets, and bringing a rural feel to the smelly, noisy, crowded town, were orchards, gardens and even a few fields, and, in the north-west angle of the city walls, an area of allotment-like plots known as 'the Crofts'.

In sharp contrast to the splendid residences of the well-to-do were the dwellings of the poor, who frequently lived in crowded conditions in cellars, behind shops, or in poorer districts such as the area around Gloverstone.

In the north-east angle, almost a fifth of the area within the city walls was occupied by the cathedral, its close containing the homes of the clergy and associated buildings. Since medieval times spiritual power had been counter-balanced by the secular, in the shape of the castle, which occupied a similarly large area in the south-west corner of the walls.

Like most of England's medieval towns, seventeenth-century Chester had spread beyond the confines of its city walls. Suburbs had grown up: to the east along Foregate, or Forest Street, as far as the tollgate known as the 'Bars' and the village of Boughton; to the north along Northgate Street: and below the city walls along St John's and Cow Lanes.

Along the banks of the River Dee were the establishments of the leather workers and the famous water mills. There were eleven of the latter, six of them for corn milling, and three for cloth fulling, whilst the remaining two were employed in raising water from the river to the water tower which had been built over the Watergate in 1600 by John Tyrer. From here, and from another tower at Boughton springs, east of the city, water was piped to various properties and to a conduit situated at the Cross in the town centre.[5]

The medieval Dee Bridge linked Chester with the suburb of Handbridge, situated on the rising ground on the west bank of the river. Home of the Dee fishermen, Handbridge had frequently been destroyed and rebuilt during medieval conflicts with the Welsh.

Clearly visible from the west bank of the Dee were the spires and towers of Chester's eight churches. Particularly noticeable was St John's, some 150 yards to the east of the city walls, whose dominating tower would prove a sore trial to Chester's garrison during the later stages of the siege.

Chester was still closely surrounded by countryside. The townfields, where cattle were grazed and crops grown, lay to the north, and elsewhere the built-up areas were bounded by a mixture of heathland, cultivated ground and marshes. The latter were quite extensive, particularly towards the mouth of the Dee, and treacherous, though not impassable to those familiar with their shifting pathways. To the south-west of the city walls was a great area of open grassland, formed by the gradual retreat of the River Dee, known as the Roodeye (after a cross which had stood there), and used as a site for fairs, the embryonic Chester Races, public meetings and the grazing of livestock.[6]

Four main roads radiated out from Chester. From the Northgate ran the route which led via Hoole, Bridgetrafford and Delamere Forest to Warrington and the crossings of the Mersey. The path of the old Roman Watling Street led through the Eastgate, passing through Boughton, the Gowey Valley, Tarvin and Peckforton Gap, and on to Cheshire's second town, Nantwich, and eventually into the Midlands. Crossing Rowton Heath to the south-east of the city was the road to Whitchurch and Shrewsbury, with a branch into Wales over Farndon Bridge. Perhaps most important of all was the old soldiers' way into North Wales, leaving Chester by the Bridgegate, traversing the Dee Bridge, then tracing its course through Wrexham, Hawarden and the moors and hills beyond, with a fork diverging along the Flintshire coast.

3. Eighteenth-century view of Chester from the south west. Note the castle (centre), Dee Bridge and cathedral (centre left). The dominating tower of St John's Church is to the right of the castle.

On three of these roads lay what was in effect the 'outer ring' of Chester's defences. Beeston Castle, built by the thirteenth-century earls of Chester, from its towering and precipitous rocky crag dominated the Cheshire Plain and Peckforton Gap.[7] King Edward I's castle of Hawarden, 7 miles west of Chester, was the first of the chain of fortifications which studded North Wales, whilst the Welsh end of Farndon Bridge was secured by Holt Castle. Though possession of these strongholds was not always essential for use of the routes which they guarded, their occupation for much of the war by the Royalists was a significant advantage to the defenders of Chester.

Chester was not only the administrative centre of the County Palatine; it had also been a bishopric since 1541 and was an important centre of ecclesiastical government.

Chester's economic well-being was closely linked with its surrounding region. Numerous fairs were held, at which county gentry, their wives, and prospering Chester mercantile families rubbed shoulders with apprentices, Cheshire farmers and cattle drovers from North Wales, and the lilting tones of the Welsh were as commonly heard as the slower speech of the Cheshire Lowlands. The main industries of the town were connected with the cloth and leather trades, the latter estimated to have employed 25% of the working population.[8] Chester-produced goods were sold over a wide area, and the city was of great importance to the economy of North Wales, importing cattle, lead and coal.

The civil government of Chester had been established under the Charter of 1547, and was administered by an assembly consisting of the mayor, two sheriffs, a recorder, twenty-four aldermen and sixty elected common councillors, chosen by the householders of the city. In practice, the mayor, recorder, sheriffs and aldermen exercised the real authority, and formed a kind of 'inner cabinet' known as the 'Brethren'. The mayor was elected annually in a somewhat complex process supposed to reflect the generalised view of the citizens.[9]

It has been suggested that Chester came into the hands of the Royalists as the result of manoeuvrings by a small group of aldermen determined to retain pre-war trading advantages which they had obtained from the Crown, and had since maintained and extended by sometimes dubious means. However, by the 1640s, threats to trade and Chester's decline as a port in the face of Liverpool, her brash new rival on the Mersey, were causing more generalised unease. Also significant was the sharp rise in pro-Royalist sentiment through much of the region as Civil War loomed.[10] In any case, the Brethren, among whose number were the leading merchants and employers of the city, had ample means to gain the support of the generally acquiescent common councillors and ordinary citizens, whose livelihood depended upon Chester's prosperity.

Aldermen and sheriffs were not elected, vacancies being filled by co-opted members chosen by the remainder of the Brethren. Finances were obtained by means of the assembly's powers to collect money to pay for the administration of the city, and by its right to administer the estates of minors and orphans within Chester and its 'liberties' (the surrounding area beyond the city walls).

The trade of Chester was controlled by the 'Guild Merchant', whose presiding officer was usually the mayor, so that it and the civil government of the city were normally in the same hands. The Guild could own property, hold courts, and fine and even imprison offenders. By the seventeenth century the Guild was a 'closed shop', an oligarchy of a few wealthy families who regulated trade to their own advantage, and stifled the opposition of any dissidents. Its powers were secured by an annual payment of £300 to the Crown.

Among the leading supporters of the King were a group of local magnates, including Lord Rivers, Lord Kilmorrey and the Earl of Derby, all of whom had substantial holdings of property in and around Chester. Derby was lord lieutenant of the county, and although the main family estates lay across the Mersey in Lancashire, his influence (or, in the summer of 1642, for practical purposes that of his son, Lord Strange, soon to be 7th Earl of Derby) was considerable.

Of more immediate significance were the attitudes of the Chester merchants and assembly members. Chief among them were two cousins, William and Francis Gamull. The Gamulls had wide-ranging commercial interests. They were exporters of calf skins, leather merchants, and landowners, and also possessed six of the Dee mills, with fishing rights on the river. The Gamulls were hard-headed businessmen, who lost no opportunity to extend their

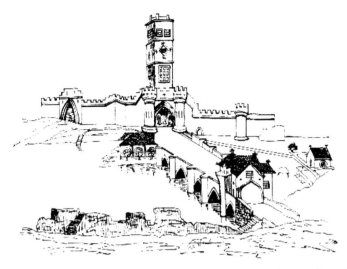

4. Dee Mills and Dee Bridge. Based on a contemporary drawing by Randle Holme, this view shows some of the Dee Mills close to the Dee Bridge, and the gatehouse at its southern end. The water tower on the Bridgegate (centre) is wrongly positioned. As other illustrations make clear, it was actually smaller and built above the left-hand tower. On the far left is the little-used Shipgate.

empire. They made full use of advantages such as those presented to them by Francis's election in 1634 as mayor, and in 1641 as a member of Parliament for Chester. The Gamulls' acquisition of exclusive trading privileges by royal grant, or by more clandestine means, made them highly unpopular among many rivals and ordinary citizens, but by virtue of being among the largest employers in Chester, the Gamulls, with their fine house on Bridge Street, were assured of considerable power within the city.

The Holme family were also influential Royalists. Father and son, both named Randle, were deputies of the College of Heralds, and important members of the Painters, Glaziers, Emblazoners and Stationers Company. Randle Holme II was mayor in 1643–44, and author of a picturesque and detailed account of the siege.[11]

Other leading Royalists included the Aldersley and Bavand families, who were prominent in the Irish trade. Charles Walley, mayor in the later part of the war, was an innkeeper and merchant, with several properties in the city. Also noted as supporters of the Crown were two other mayors of the period, Thomas Cowper and William Ince (the recorder), Robert Brerewood, and John and Colonel Robert Werden, with estates just outside the city.

Religion was an important factor in events leading to the outbreak of war. The majority of the citizens of Chester were Anglican, but, partly because of

5. Sir William Brereton (1604–61). The most committed Cheshire Parliamentarian activist, Brereton's opposition to the King and his supporters in Chester seems to have been motivated partly by pre-war trading disputes as well as by religious and political conviction. Despite the image presented by this portrait, Brereton's abilities were more marked as an administrator than a field commander.

the city's links with Ireland, there was also a significant Catholic element. Both of these groups were generally pro-Royalist. It was from the numerically small but influential Puritan section of the population that most Parliamentarian support was drawn.

The openly declared Parliamentarian party within Chester was relatively small in number. Leader of the Puritan faction in the assembly was William Edwards, an ironmonger and ex-mayor, who came originally from Flintshire. Edwards was a business rival of the Gamulls, and had been worsted by them in the courts prior to the war, and this may well have influenced his choice of allegiance. Among his main supporters were the Brien family of nearby Brien Stapleford. None of them had any real influence over political developments in Chester; they were outweighed by the pro-Royalist majority, and eventually had to flee to Parliamentarian-held territory.

Throughout the war the dominating figure among the Cheshire Parliamentarians, and Royalist Chester's greatest foe, was Sir William Brereton. Born in 1604 at Handforth in the north-east of the county, Brereton was a noted Puritan, married to Susannah, daughter of Cheshire's other leading, but Presbyterian, Parliamentarian, Sir George Booth of Dunham Massy. Brereton was created a baronet in 1627, and in 1634 travelled widely in Britain and the Low Countries, where it has been suggested that he may have gained some brief military experience. Possibly, however, he saw no action prior to the Civil War, and indeed his apparent lack of military training was to be remarked upon by Brereton's enemies, both Royalist and Parliamentarian, together with imputations of personal cowardice. These latter accusations are not supported by direct evidence, although it is fair to describe Brereton's skills as being more those of planner and administrator than combat commander.

Sir William seems to have gained the reputation of having a somewhat vengeful nature. He had business interests in Chester, and owned a town house there. A fairly ruthless businessman himself, Brereton had been thwarted in some of his commercial enterprises by the Chester authorities, incited by the Gamulls, and his political convictions were no doubt sharpened by a desire to obtain restitution.

Also influential in pre-war Chester politics, having a somewhat uneasy relationship with the citizens, was the ecclesiastical circle around the bishop, John Bridgeman. They were led by the bishop's son, Orlando Bridgeman, MP for Wigan. Although Bridgeman was absent from Chester for much of the war, he played an important role in organising Royalist support and supplies, especially for the English troops from Ireland who arrived in 1643–44.

These then were some of the leading personalities, but the main burden of the hardships of the years ahead would fall upon the humbler citizens – the 'meaner sort' as they were known. Their attitudes towards the coming of war are largely obscure, and in truth they had little opportunity to make their views known. Until almost the end, they had no option but to follow the course set for them by their leaders.

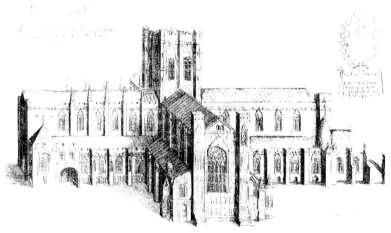

6. Chester Cathedral (St Werburgh's) in 1656. This contemporary view depicts the cathedral as it appeared prior to extensive nineteenth-century restoration. Despite a frequently uneasy relationship with the citizens of Chester, the bishop and his circle had an influential role.

As hopes of a peaceful settlement of the nation's difficulties died during the early summer of 1642, the thoughts of both sides turned increasingly to military matters. The English Civil War is often thought of, wrongly, as a contest between two amateur armies, who learnt the art of war as they went along. But in 1642 the British Isles contained large numbers of men experienced in warfare. They had fought in the series of European conflicts known collectively as the Thirty Years' War, and nearer home they had seen service in Ireland and in the Scots Wars of 1639 and 1640. There was a hard core of professional soldiers available as the nucleus of the officer corps which both sides required as the basic framework of their armies, and King and Parliament vied eagerly for their services.

Most of the male population had at least some rudimentary military knowledge because of their liability to serve in the Trained Bands and militia – the local defence forces maintained by each county and city. Though standards of training and equipment varied widely, at least something was provided, and could be brought up to an adequate level of military competence surprisingly quickly.

Another popular image which should be dispelled is that of the be-ribboned, swaggering aristocratic 'Cavalier', locked in combat with the austere, psalm-singing, plebian 'Roundhead'. Although such sterotypes did exist, and it is true to say that Royalist cavalry regiments included a somewhat higher proportion of the nobility and gentry than did their opponents, the reality was that both armies consisted of a remarkably similar cross-section of the population. The cavalry of both sides, for example, hardly surprisingly at a time when the vast majority of the male population had at least adequate skills in horsemanship, included troopers from every walk of life. Whilst the Parliamentarian horse might indeed include examples of what Cromwell called 'a plain russet-coated captain that knows what he fights for, and loves what he knows', the same was equally true of his opponents, whose ranks included horse-dealers, choirmasters and play actors!

A mid-seventeenth-century army consisted of four basic elements: horse, dragoons, foot and artillery. In order better to understand events during the siege of Chester we should briefly examine each of them.

The cavalry, or 'horse', as they were usually known, were still regarded as the élite of the battlefield, though their supremacy was being challenged increasingly by the infantry, or 'foot'. In theory an army should have included one horseman for every two foot soldiers, though in practice this proportion was rarely maintained. The Royalist armies, for example, tended to have a consistently higher percentage of horse. The type of cavalry most commonly employed in the

7. Cavalry (from Cruso, *Militarie Instructions for the Cavalrie*, 1635). These troopers (or 'Harquebusiers') are fully equipped with pot helmet, back and breast plates, sword, pistols and carbine. Such standards of perfection were not always reached, particularly in regional forces in the earlier stages of the Civil War.

English Civil War were known as 'harquebusiers'. Ideally the harquebusier would be equipped with a buff coat of hardened leather or hide, back and breast plates and 'pot' helmet, and be armed with sword, pair of pistols and carbine. In practice, especially during the earlier stages of the war, this was rarely achieved.

But by about mid-1643 the average trooper of horse on each side would have appeared virtually identical and would have been equipped at least partially in the recommended fashion. In most cases the only way of distinguishing between Royalist and Parliamentarian would have been by the colour of sash (frequently crimson for the Royalists and orange for their opponents), or different identifying field signs, such as pieces of white paper in their hatbands, or sprigs of plants, which the soldiers often wore.

The theoretical strength of a regiment of horse was about 500 men, though actual numbers varied widely. In the earlier stages of the war, the Royalist horse had a definite qualitative 'edge' over their opponents, but by the time they became a significant factor in operations around Chester (in 1644–45) that superiority had largely disappeared, and the two sides were fairly equally matched.

Because of the nature of siege warfare, set-piece cavalry actions, with a few notable exceptions such as the battle of Rowton Heath, were relatively rare events during the operations around Chester. Much more common was the use of small parties of horse in raids to beat up enemy quarters, seize supplies and intimidate the surrounding countryside.[12]

The middle and late seventeenth century saw a steady increase in the importance of infantry, resulting from improved firearms, training and tactics. A regiment of foot theoretically totalled 1,200 men, in ten companies, with a

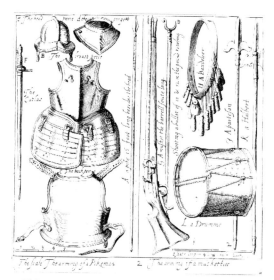

8. Infantry equipment. This contemporary engraving shows on the left the recommended arms and body armour of a pikeman. In practice the armour, other than sometimes a headpiece, was little used in the Civil War. Musket rests, shown here on the right, also went out of use as lighter firearms were introduced. The partisan (right) was frequently carried by officers and NCOs. The halberd (far right) was particularly useful in close-quarter infantry combat.

recommended ratio of one pikeman to two musketeers. In practice, the proportions varied widely according to circumstances and the views of individual commanders.

The pike, because of its antiquity, was traditionally seen as the more honourable weapon of the foot soldier. In theory a pike should have been 16–18ft in length, but was frequently shortened to about 12ft for greater ease in carrying. Pikemen also carried a poor quality sword, used more for brawling, chopping firewood and terrorising civilians than in actual combat.

Though in theory pikemen were equipped with armour – including back and breast plates, tassets to protect the thighs and an iron headpiece – in actuality armour was progressively less used by both sides. In battle, pikes were employed in mass formations, both to fend off enemy horse, and, when fighting their own kind, in a tactic known as 'push of pike', which in some ways resembled a modern rugby scrum, in which the massed pikes attempted to disorder their opponents, knock them off their feet or push them back, in an action which was often quite bloodless unless one side was routed. In siege warfare pikemen were of limited use, and their pikes were often replaced with halberds or other more easily handled pole-type weapons.

Musketeers not only made up at least two thirds of the strength of the average foot regiment, but they also bore an increasingly large share of the

9. Pikemen. These pikemen on campaign, with minimal body armour, are typical of those employed by both sides in the Civil War.

fighting. The standard firearm of the Civil War musketeer was the matchlock, a considerably more effective weapon than sometimes suggested. Though it had a theoretical range of 600 yards, the matchlock was more commonly used at a range of 100 yards or less. It had the advantage of simplicity and robust construction, and was cheap to produce, though unreliable in wet and windy conditions, when the length of match used to fire it might be extinguished.

Although military manuals laid down lengthy loading and firing procedures, in action these were considerably simplified, so that a musket might be loaded and fired in approximately thirty seconds. Musketeers also carried the same type of cheap sword as the pike men, though in hand-to-hand fighting they preferred to make use of their musket butts. Various methods were used to carry ammunition, including a bandolier, carrying about twelve tin or wooden powder chargers. Also used, particularly by the Royalist forces, were powder bags, carried at the waist by means of a belt. In other cases, cartridges might simply be stuffed into the soldiers' pockets.

Firelock or flintlock muskets, more complicated and expensive, but also more reliable, were sometimes used to equip special companies of élite troops, such as the 'firelocks' who originally served with the Royalist forces from Ireland, but ended up as Sir William Brereton's crack soldiers in the fighting around Chester.

There were various formations and drills for the employment of musketeers en masse in set-piece battles. At Chester most fighting was small-scale in nature, with both sides increasingly employing the company as the basic tactical unit, mixing contingents from several regiments in special 'task forces' as required.

Dragoons were basically mounted infantry, employed by both sides around Chester for scouting, raiding and clearing enemy outposts. They were usually equipped with a short-barrelled musket, or carbine, and sword.[13]

Artillery was less used in battle during the English Civil War than on the Continent. However its value in siege warfare was paramount.

There were various schemes for classifying the types of guns in use, with a colourful array of names, ranging from the massive full cannon firing a shot of 63lb weight, through culverins, demi-culverins, sakers, minions, falconets and drakes, the latter a three-pounder or less. Also used to considerable effect during the siege of Chester was the mortar, which will be described later. In practice the real division was between siege artillery, the heavy guns from full cannon to culverin, and the lighter pieces which were more generally employed in battle.

As with the musket, much has been made of the slow rate of fire and inaccuracy of Civil War artillery, but again this is based on a not-necessarily-correct assumption that the cumbersome procedures of the drill book were actually

10. Musketeer. This fully equipped musketeer, with matchlock, musket rest, bandolier carrying about a dozen wooden or tin powder charge containers, powder flask and cheap sword, could have served with the forces of either side, although his 'montero' style cap was particularly popular in the Royalist armies.

11. Artillery. Commonly employed types of artillery: cannon (top) and culverin (below). Note the firing platforms of timber or woven branches, intended to minimise the tendency of guns to become embedded in the ground on recoil after firing.

followed in the field. Artillery was difficult and expensive to move, and its high consumption of often scarce supplies of gunpowder was a constant headache to commanders.[14]

Both sides recognised the desirability of providing uniform dress for their troops, but this proved difficult in reality. Though at the start of the war a wide variety of coat colours were worn, as the war went on red and blue became more commonly used, though by no means universal. Many troops, especially in outlying areas away from the main centres of production, never received uniforms at all, and wore civilian clothing for considerable periods. This was certainly true, at least for their opening campaign, of many of the troops brought over from Ireland in 1643–44.

It was partly in order to overcome this problem, as well as to provide rallying points and a certain *esprit de corps*, that flags were used. In theory each regiment had a set of flags following a recognised system, but again there was much variation in practice.

The men who fought for King or Parliament did so from a variety of motives. Many who enlisted in the opening stages of the war were more or less volunteers, joining either from personal belief or in hopes of regular pay, loot and excitement. Others, of course, went to the wars less willingly, either, as in the case with the city regiment at Chester, at the behest of masters or employers or later as a result of conscription.

12. Dragoon and camp follower. Dragoons were basically mounted infantry.
The women who accompanied Civil War armies, despite spasmodic attempts by authority
to limit their numbers, occupied a wide spectrum from wives or others in established
relationships through traders of various kinds to whores (or 'leaguer ladies').

As the war became prolonged, most of the bright hopes of the early volunteers were speedily disillusioned. Soldiers were irregularly paid, if at all, and free quarter, whereby they were maintained at the cost of local civilians, with whom they were billeted, was resorted to. Loot and excitement also came the soldier's way much less frequently than had perhaps been expected. Instead disease, and to a lesser extent casualties in action, took a terrible toll. The fate of the sick and injured was frequently a grim one, as medical and surgical care was often rudimentary.

By 1644 both sides were employing conscription, though the citizens of Chester itself, apart from service in Gamull's regiment, were theoretically exempt. In many cases, conscription was seen by local authorities as an opportunity to rid themselves of troublesome elements in their communities, and desertion was rife.

Not to be forgotten is the part played in the war by women. Thousands of wives and more irregular 'camp-followers' accompanied their men on campaign. Chester will have seen many such, often Welsh or Irish, and the women and children of the city would be caught up in the action and terror of the later stages of the siege.

2

WAR COMES TO CHESTER: AUGUST 1642–JULY 1643

There were many causes for the wars that convulsed the British Isles from 1638 onwards. Though religious, political and economic tensions had been growing for many years, matters were brought to a head by the beliefs and actions of King Charles I, which increasingly set him on a collision course with powerful elements of his subjects, especially as represented in Parliament.

A central pillar of Charles' philosophy of government was his belief in the Divine Right of Kings, phrased in his uncompromising fashion as 'Princes are not bound to give account of their actions but to God alone.' This belief inevitably led to an increasingly centralised type of government, with power focused on the King himself and a close circle of advisers, and which soon encountered difficulties. The first of these was financial. In contrast to the steadily increasing wealth of the gentry and mercantile classes, whose increasing power and influence was mirrored in their domination of the House of Commons, the monarchy had been growing poorer. Its financial burdens were increased during the 1620s by a disastrous foreign policy which led to growing discord between King and Parliament. The latter, on the whole strongly conservative, hearkened back nostalgically to the retrospectively rosy days of Good Queen Bess, and condemned what many of its members saw as the King's lack of support for the Protestant cause in the religious conflicts gripping Europe.

In 1629 Charles dissolved Parliament, and embarked upon an eleven-year period of 'personal rule'. Thanks to some unorthodox, and legally questionable, methods of tax-raising such as the notorious 'Ship Money', this functioned

13. King Charles I (1600–49). Through a fatal mixture of weakness and stubborn adherence to deeply-held but untenable beliefs, Charles did much to hasten the outbreak of Civil War.

reasonably well for a time. But there was no financial surplus available to meet unexpected emergencies, and Charles proceeded to bring about such a crisis by his religious policy which alienated more radical protestants.

Matters came to a head in 1638, with the disastrously mistaken attempt to impose the reformed English Prayer Book in Scotland. The result was a popular uprising north of the border. An attempt in 1639 by the King's government to impose a solution by force met with a humiliating reverse, as did a renewed attempt, known as the Second Scots War, in the following year. With part of northern England under occupation by a Scottish army, the King was forced to call a new Parliament to provide money to buy off the Scots.

The 'Long Parliament', which met for the first time on 3 November 1640, was determined to bring about sweeping constitutional reforms and to shift the balance of power away from the King towards Parliament. Initially it was broadly supported by the majority of influential interest groups within the country, even by many who would later be prominent Royalists. Unease was increased a year later by the outbreak of rebellion in Ireland, for it was widely, though erroneously, believed that the Irish Confederate rebels had the sympathy of the King.

Throughout 1641 tension heightened, with Parliament steadily passing legislation reducing royal powers, the King doing all he could to prevent this, and both sides taking a progressively harder line. In January 1642 Charles failed in an attempt to arrest his leading opponents, and from then on Civil War was virtually inevitable. But increasingly radical demands by Parliament, and the King's success in portraying the potential consequences of the social anarchy which might result from the victory of his opponents, led to a marked pro-Royalist reaction in many parts of the country. When the Royal Standard was raised on 22 August at Nottingham, formalising the outbreak of war, the two sides were more equally matched than might have been expected.

As friction between the King and his various opponents grew in the years before the outbreak of war, uneasiness and disquiet became apparent even in areas seemingly as far removed from the centre of events as Chester.

The brief Scots wars caused alarm throughout the north of England. Although Chester was some distance from the scene of hostilities, on 8 September 1640 the authorities ordered repairs to the city gates and a watch to be kept at night. Like most English cities and towns, following a century and a half of relative internal peace, Chester was unprepared for war. On 18 October 1640, the assembly approved a series of orders, in view of the 'warlike and dangerous times', to remedy the 'great want of arms' in Chester. Back and breast plates, muskets, calivers and halberds were ordered, and Francis Gamull was appointed captain of the city Trained Band.[1]

The English Trained Bands, drawn in general from the more substantial members of the community, and used by government partly for internal security, and the militia, in which all males between sixteen and sixty were theoretically liable for service, are generally rated poorly by historians. Indeed their showing during the Civil War was often unimpressive, though there were exceptions. Whilst not amongst the best, the Cheshire Trained Bands, which included those of Chester, were somewhat better than average. Lord Derby, as lord lieutenant, and some of the other county gentry had shown an interest in improving their efficiency, and had paid for professional instructors.

The normal strength of the Chester Trained Band seems to have been one company of about 100 men. In 1613 the part-time members included one carpenter, three maltsters, seven tanners, seven bakers, six hatmakers, six butchers, three drapers, thirteen shoemakers, five glovers and seven tailors.[2] In 1639 their officers were Captain Dutton, Lieutenant William Maxey and Ensign Jacob, all professional soldiers, who were paid £5 10s.[3] The somewhat homespun character of the Trained Bands is suggested by an entry in the City Treasurer's Accounts for 1638/9: 'A quart of sack and cakes in the Pentice when Mr Mayor and Sir Thomas Smith came from viewing of the city soldiers, 1s 4d.'[4] The Pentice was a timber building attached to the end of St

Peter's Church near the Town Cross, used for storing the arms and equipment of the Trained Bands.

In theory work on improving Chester's defences continued into the summer of 1641; on 1 June orders were given for a general assessment of the inhabitants in order to pay for repairs to the walls. Added impetus was given by the outbreak in October of the Irish Rebellion. Rumours of 'papist' conspiracies, and exaggerated tales of atrocities by the rebels, together with the unpopular presence in the city of troops bound for Ireland, all served to raise the political temperature. Added to this were the existing animosities between the various factions in Chester. As well as disputes between Sir William Brereton and the city authorities, there was also friction and rivalry between the Gamulls and William Edwards, which caused Edwards to accuse the Gamulls of placing their own interests above those of the city. Whatever the truth of this, it ensured that they would be on opposing sides when war came.

In July 1642 a general assembly of Chester citizens declared their opposition to the imminent war, but the first moves in the city had begun even before the King raised his standard. On 8 August, Sir William Brereton and William Edwards attempted to 'beat the drum' for recruits for the Parliamentarian forces. A 'great tumult' resulted, with the citizens summoned to arms by the mayor, and Brereton and his associates were disarmed. Although Sir William himself was allowed to leave the city, his followers were imprisoned for a time.[5]

However this did not mean that Chester was committed to the Royalist cause, indeed popular enthusiasm for either side was lukewarm. Because of this, when, on 6 September, further sums were levied for the repair of the gates and walls, this was not ostensibly in support of either King or Parliament, but 'because of dangerous times'.[6]

King Charles was well aware of the importance of securing Chester, and after his arrival at Shrewsbury, where the Royalist field army was mustering, he paid a flying visit to the city on 23 September. Charles was received with considerable ceremony, and, escorted by musketeers of the Trained Band, was met at Boughton by the Sheriffs and their officers, dressed in scarlet. The King entered the city to the sound of church bells and trumpets, and salutes of musketry from the Trained Bands and levies which the local gentry had raised for the field army.

The Recorder, Robert Brerewood, delivered a loyal address, but of more immediate value to the financially-pressed monarch was a 'gift' of £300 in gold. This was apparently a smaller amount than had been expected, and the authorities also declined a royal request that the Trained Band be sent to join the field army. While adopting a generally conciliatory approach during his short visit, and making no attempt to enforce unpopular demands, Charles ensured the election as mayor of the pro-Royalist William Ince. He briefly arrested and removed from Chester some suspected Parliamentarian supporters, and confiscated their property. On his departure, on 28 September, the King took with him the newly raised regiments of Sir Edward Fitton, Earl Rivers and Sir Thomas Aston, seriously weakening Royalist strength in the area.[7]

Chester was finally secured for the Royalists on 21 October, when the assembly ordered 'that for the defence of the city 300 men, inhabitants of the City should be raised [in addition to the Trained Band] and that they should be armed with muskets and their appurtenances.' Sixty-one citizens were named as agreeing to supply between one and three muskets each, and 'Mr Mayor, Mr Recorder and the rest of his brethren were to consult on how the remainder of the 300 muskets were to be raised.'[8]

This order was the origin of Francis Gamull's City Regiment, although he was not formally commissioned as its colonel until March 1643. The manpower of the regiment, though all were nominally volunteers at this stage, included a large proportion of men directly or indirectly beholden for their jobs and homes to the leaders of the Royalist faction. Most of the officers were recruited from Chester merchant families and the local gentry. Eventually reaching a strength of 800 men, and probably a mainly musketeer unit, the unit was intended primarily for the defence of Chester (indeed, theoretically exempt from serving outside its 'boundaries'). But Gamull's Redcoats were also an ideal instrument to ensure the Brethren's control of the city.[9]

During the autumn, with the growing prospect of a long war, further defensive measures were initiated. Command in Chester was at this time exercised by the Brethren in the assembly and by a council, meeting in the Bishop's Palace, consisting of the county commissioners of array, who were leading local Royalist gentry, and including Lord Kilmorrey and Sir Edward Savage, the bishop and his son. At this stage, facing no organised opposition in the county, the Royalist task seemed fairly straightforward.

On 11 November the assembly agreed measures for keeping a constant watch in Chester. There were to be eight guards stationed at each of the six gates, two of them musketeers and two armed with halberds. A 'Court of Guard' of twelve men was to be maintained night and day at the High Cross ready to support the watch. The raw recruits were to be given intensive training: 'eight persons from the trained Bands were to be employed, four in the day and four at night, in exercising the watchmen and instructing them in the use of their arms.' The shortage of firearms is demonstrated by an order that 'The musketeers who watched at the gates and at the Cross should receive their muskets from the

Pentice and pass them on to those who succeeded them in the watch.' The cost of maintaining the guard was estimated at £66 13s 4d a month, to be raised by a levy among all inhabitants.[10]

On 6 December the assembly agreed that:

> We shall all joyne together in a mutuall Association for the defence of the Citty against all Forces whatsoever that shall come in any hostile manner for to invade the Citty or disturbe the peace thereof.[11]

The careful wording of this statement was probably intended to placate remaining neutralist sentiment within Chester. By now many Royalist gentry and their supporters from Cheshire and elsewhere had taken refuge in Chester, and it was agreed that they would take a share of the financial burden.

Events soon increased the urgency of preparations. Parliamentarian supporters overran eastern and central Cheshire, the county Trained Bands disintegrated, and the Royalists were left holding only Chester itself and the western part of the county. The collapse led to Orlando Bridgeman proposing on 22 December a local truce, the treaty of Bunbury, a move seen by both sides only as a temporary expedient to buy time.

The truce duly collapsed in January 1643, with the return of Sir William Brereton to command Parliament's forces in Cheshire, and the despatch by the King of Sir Thomas Aston as his colonel-general of Cheshire. But Aston was speedily defeated on 28 January at Nantwich.

14. Training. Provided competent instructors were available, raw recruits could be turned into adequate soldiers in the course of a few weeks.

15. Sir Thomas Aston (1600–45). A leading Cheshire royalist, Aston owed his command more to local influence than to military ability, and enjoyed little success.

Orlando Bridgeman reacted by bringing into Chester at least two regiments of foot from North Wales, totalling about 1,000 men. Aston's defeated cavalry also arrived, causing problems over the allocation of money and supplies. With the King's support, Bridgeman overruled an agreement between Aston and the county commissioners of array, and appropriated for the maintenance of the garrison the resources of Chester and its immediate area. Aston's men were reduced to plundering in order to survive.

The urgent need of funds with which to pay the increased garrison was demonstrated in February, when some of Sir Roger Mostyn's Welsh foot ran riot, and sacked Brereton's town house. It is likely that this affront was one of the reasons for Sir William's dogged determination to capture Chester, whilst fear of his vengeance stiffened the resistance of the citizens.[12]

Mostyn's regiment consisted mainly of raw recruits and inexperienced officers. Though the other Welsh foot regiment in the city was probably no better, its commander, Robert Ellice of Gwasnewydd, near Wrexham, had served with the Swedes during the Thirty Years' War, and trained as a military engineer. He was therefore seen as the best available choice to supervise the design of Chester's improved defences.[13]

16. Chester Castle. Agricola's Tower is the main surviving medieval feature of the castle, which was almost entirely rebuilt in the nineteenth century.

The existing fortifications consisted of the castle and city walls. Chester Castle included an inner and outer bailey with curtain walls, two great fortified gatehouses, and strong square towers at intervals, the whole sited to dominate the bridge across the Dee. The castle acted as royal prison for Cheshire, and its great hall and numerous other buildings provided accommodation for the administration of the County Palatine. Like most English castles away from the restless Scottish borders, the long era of comparative peace following the end of the wars of the fifteenth century had led to Chester Castle falling into some disrepair.

During the Civil War the castle would be used as a magazine, was garrisoned, and for a time served as the governor's residence. It is unclear if it underwent many repairs, but was evidently still regarded as defensible. The River Dee in any case protected it from direct assault.

The modern city walls differ considerably from their appearance at the time of the Civil War. They have been rebuilt and repaired on numerous occasions during their long history, partly because the red sandstone from which they are constructed suffers badly from weathering. By the beginning of the seventeenth century the walls were in a bad state of repair, in some places actually falling down. Full-scale repair work does not seem to have begun until early 1643. At this time new drawbridges were fitted for the Eastgate, Northgate, Bridgegate and castle. The walls had earthen ramparts or linings erected behind them to absorb the effects of bombardment, and in places the medieval ramparts were pierced with gunports.

17. Eastgate. The medieval gateway, with its twin towers, was built around the
original Roman gateway. It was demolished in the nineteenth century and
replaced by the present structure.

The main entrance to Chester was the Eastgate, a four-storey structure with
octagonal towers on either side. Moving northwards along the walls, adjacent
to the cathedral was a small postern gate originally designed to give the clergy
access to the Kaleyards, and next to it was the Saddlers' Tower, a round tower
named after the Saddlers' Company of the merchant guilds, who met there.
Severely battered during the siege, the tower was later demolished. The 200-
yard stretch of wall between the Saddlers' and Phoenix Towers was the scene
of some of the bitterest fighting of the siege. The eastern and northern sectors
of the walls were protected by a dry fosse or ditch, which, even though it had
partially collapsed in places, was a much more formidable obstacle than is
apparent today. Phoenix Tower (now known as King Charles' Tower) stands,
substantially unaltered, at the north-eastern angle of the walls.

From here the walls run westwards to the Northgate, which at that time was
also used as the city prison. Described as 'an inconvenient and unsightly pile
of buildings', it was demolished in 1807.

The next defensive position, a gun platform, was later to be known as
Morgan's Mount, although the actual 'Morgan's Mount' of the siege was part
of the outworks directly below the city walls at this point. About 80 yards
beyond is the alcove now known as Pemberton's Parlour. This is an eighteenth-century structure, replacing the Goblin Tower, which was a round
tower spanning the walls. The tower suffered heavy damage during the siege,
and was demolished in 1702. Somewhere near here, at a point now difficult to
trace, a breach was made in the walls during the latter stages of the siege.

18. Northgate. A medieval structure based on a Roman gateway.

At Bonewaldesthorne's (or the New) Tower the wall turns south, a 100ft-long spur connecting Bonewaldesthorne's Tower with the Water Tower, which was built in 1322 when the Dee covered most of what is now the Roodeye. By the seventeenth century it had been left high and dry.

The walls then run south-east to the Watergate, which was formerly the main entrance for goods landed from the Dee. This whole length of walls was without towers or other defensive positions, for the Dee made any assault impracticable.

Beyond the castle the defences continue roughly north-eastwards to the Ship Gate, probably little used, and the neighbouring Bridgegate, a formidable structure flanked by two towers, and with John Tyrer's water tower above it. The Bridgegate protected the entrance to the Dee Bridge, which at this time probably had eight arches and was defended at its Handbridge end by another gatehouse and drawbridge.

The walls continue to the Newgate. This stretch was dominated by the tower of St John's Church, and witnessed severe bombardment and fighting. Traces of the impact of cannon shot can still be seen on Barnaby's Tower. The Newgate was rebuilt in 1608, and is the only surviving original gateway from the time of the siege. Now called the Wolfgate, it stands beside the modern New Gate.

Beyond the Newgate, the short stretch of wall linking it with the Eastgate and completing the circuit included Thimbley's Tower, which was also severely damaged during the fighting.[14]

19. Castle and Bridgegate. In this eighteenth-century view the structures on the riverbank below the castle are connected with the tanning industry. The water tower and St John's Church are clearly visible.

Work on the outworks protecting the suburbs began around February 1643, when Ellice and Major Humphrey Sydenham, a veteran of the fighting in Ireland,

> Caused according to the modern way of fortification to be cut a trench and [a] mudwall to be made from Deeside without the Bars to Deeside at the new tower, the wall to be repaired and lined with earth and turnpikes at all the outworks as Barrs, Cowlane end, without the Northgate and at the Mount at Dee lane end, by Little st Johns, besides severall mounts, pit falls and other devices to secure the outworks and annoy the enemy's approach to the city.[15]

Thomas Cowper in an account, written in 1769, based on documents since lost, describes the extent of the defences.

> The Outworks began about the middle of that part of the City Walls which lies about the New tower (looking towards Hawarden) and the Northgate, and proceeding towards the Stone Bridge leading towards Blacon inclined then to the North East and took in the utmost limits of the further Northgate Street then turning Eastward near Flookersbrook encompassed Horn Lane, the Jousting Croft, and all that part of the Town to Boughton whence the works were carried down to the Brink of the River.[16]

20. Construction of defences. Soldiers and civilian forced labour were used to carry out the plans of the military engineers.

The defences followed a common European design, consisting of an earth rampart (the curtain) designed to absorb artillery fire, linking up a series of salients intended to provide flanking fire and a number of mounts designed to hold cannon. The 'falls' which Randle Holme mentions were pits with stakes in them, like those sometimes employed by hunters, which were covered with brushwood. The turnpikes were the gates where roads entered the outworks, which themselves were probably topped off with palisades and 'stormpoles' (sharpened stakes protruding at an angle from the outer face of the earthworks).[17]

There were two main weaknesses in the outworks as they were originally constructed. One was their sheer length, totalling over 2 miles. Normally only the mounts and redoubts would actually be garrisoned, but the manpower needed to defend them adequately was greater than available. The second weakness was a great salient constructed in order to include Flookersbrook Hall within the defences. The main reason for this, and perhaps for the extent of the outworks as a whole, was the unwillingness of the citizens to see any of their property destroyed.

As the war dragged on into the spring of 1643, so Chester became steadily more vital to the Royalist cause. The decision to appoint a military governor seems to have been taken largely on the initiative of Orlando Bridgeman, though the Royalist high command in Oxford must also have been concerned by the deteriorating military position in Cheshire. The first governor (appointed on 14 March 1643) was responsible to and paid by the city authorities, though recommended by the King, and detached from the Royalist 'Oxford' Army. Sir Nicholas Byron, an Essex man, was a professional soldier, described as a 'person of great affability and dexterity as well as martiall knowledge.' Byron had fought in Europe, served in the Scots Wars and commanded a brigade of foot at Edgehill.[18]

The role of governor needs some explanation, though his powers, especially it would seem in Chester, were not always clear even to contemporaries. All military units in the garrison, and measures for its defence, came under the governor, who, if he were the King's representative, also had ultimate control over civilian matters. Most governors normally acted as far as possible through the civil authorities, without whose co-operation effective control was difficult. In reality, a great deal depended upon the personalities of individual governors, and the circumstances under which they were acting. Obviously, a town under direct threat was under much tighter control than somewhere under less pressure. Chester, like many other towns, had, in general, poor relations with its governors, as civilian and military needs came into conflict. This was probably exacerbated by none of the governors being local men. Sir Nicholas Byron, perhaps because he was responsible to the assembly, was initially less resented, though once military pressure mounted he would eventually regard his situation as untenable.

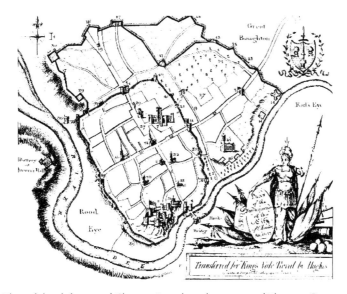

21. Plan of the defences of Chester. Based on the papers of Thomas Cowper, this illustration shows the outworks of Chester at their greatest extent in 1643. Note the 'mounts' or forts at intervals and the large amount of cultivated land included within the outworks, whose extent made them difficult to defend.

Matters were further complicated by a confused command position. Sir Thomas Aston suffered another serious reverse on 14 March at Middlewich, and lost his command. He was replaced as colonel-general of Cheshire by Sir Nicholas Byron, who was in turn responsible to the King's newly appointed lieutenant-general for North Wales and the border counties, Arthur, Lord Capel. Byron also retained his post as governor of Chester, and was placed in the unenviable position of trying to serve two masters with frequently conflicting interests.

Sir Nicholas pressed for more resources to be devoted to Chester, and felt that if the King were to be defeated in the south:

> Shrewsbury and Chester must be our last refuge, and so to provide for them in time as no thought of quitting them must be entertained.[19]

Work on the defences continued. On 3 February the assembly ordered that £500 should be levied 'from the Citizens and Inhabitants towards making the fortifications', and further assessments were to be made for the payment of the garrison.[20]

By 1 June, Sir William Brereton was writing to the Speaker of the House of Commons:

> The fortifications are as strong as the judgement and art of those men that command there can contrive them; their preparation of ordnance is

22. The Roodeye. Now Chester racecourse, and of greater extent than in the seventeenth century, when it was used for mass meetings of citizens as well as for the grazing of livestock. The stump of the cross from which it took its name is just visible (centre).

23. Arthur, Lord Capel (1610?–49). As lieutenant-general in the Welsh Marches, Capel proved to be an undistinguished officer, possibly hindered by his not being a local man.

suitable thereto, there being no less than forty cannons as we have heard and the Castle victualled for three years… Some of them in their letters which I have seen affirmed this city impregnable.[21]

Brereton's assessment of Chester's strength was exaggerated; the Royalists in reality were seriously concerned, as the Parliamentarians steadily gained ground in the surrounding area, whilst there were fears of treachery within the city itself.

On 5 June, all males not already serving with Gamull's regiment were ordered to muster on the Roodeye next day at noon, 'then and there to be enlisted, and put under such commanders as the Mayor and Governor of the city shall appoint.'[22] One month later, on 5 July, the citizens' concern took more tangible shape in the decision to send Alderman Charles Whalley and Sheriff Johnson to Oxford to 'solicit His Majesty concerning the affairs of the City.'[23]

At about the same time Sir Nicholas Byron was recalled to Oxford to resume command of his brigade of foot for the summer campaign. The deputy governor, who took over in his absence, was Sir Abraham Shipman, a Nottinghamshire-born professional soldier.[24]

Sir William Brereton, who had recently taken Stafford in a surprise attack, was encouraged to attempt to repeat his success at Chester. On 18 July, Brereton, William Edwards and 'Diverse fugitive citizens', together with

Brereton's troops, appeared outside Chester. They occupied the village of Boughton, and from the cover of some barns opened fire on the Royalist outworks, 'from which place they continued all Tuesday and Wednesday, pelting with small shot.' Next day (Tuesday 21 July) the Parliamentarians made a half-hearted assault on the outworks at Cow Lane, but this proved only to be a diversion to cover their retreat to Tarvin, leaving a few musketeers in the barns to act as a rearguard.[25]

The Royalists were encouraged by this success, which seems only to have cost them a couple of men – 'Richard Morris, butcher, shot at Boughton' and 'Allen Thompson a soldier wounded at Boughton', who died a day or so later. Morris at least was probably of Gamull's regiment.[26]

As the Parliamentarians withdrew, the garrison,

> fired all the barns without the Turnpikes at Boughton, pulled down to the ground the chappell there and the stone barn against it, ruinated all the houses there, cut down the trees, and so levelled the hedges as the rebels could have no shelter on that side.[27]

A further incident occurred next day, when:

> about seventeen or twenty of the rebels made an alarme at the Turnpike gate at Cowlane end, and shot for a while very violently, but were answered so briskly by our marksmen as three of them fell upon the place, which made the rest to fly.[28]

All of this led to growing fears in Chester of a renewed enemy assault, and at the assembly of 20 October a number of important decisions were made. A renewed petition was to be sent to the King requesting financial assistance towards the support of the garrison; three troops of horse were to be raised, and the inhabitants of various outlying districts were ordered to bring themselves, their cattle and all food supplies into the city, on pain of being 'reputed and proceeded against as adherents to the rebels and enemies to his Majesty.'[29]

These preparations proved well-timed, for the first great storm was about to burst over Royalist Chester.

3

'THE TYMES' TROUBLESOMENESSE': JULY 1643–NOVEMBER 1644

Although Brereton's first probes against Chester had failed, and the city's bells were rung in a celebratory peal, the attacks gave notice that the threat was increasing. In response further precautions were ordered, including the raising of three troops of horse to reinforce Chester's garrison. Neighbouring townships were told to send supplies of corn, cattle and other provisions, and instructions given regarding the action to be taken in the event of a surprise attack on Chester, especially at night. Citizens were to have lanterns ready, women and children were to stay indoors, and all males not enlisted in Gamull's regiment were to make their way to the Pentice, where they would be issued with weapons.[1]

The need for alertness was demonstrated early in November when the Royalists faced their most serious crisis yet. On 7 November Brereton, with Parliament's designated commander in North Wales, Sir Thomas Myddleton, launched a sudden attack on that hitherto unaffected area. They hoped to overrun north-eastern Wales and isolate Chester, bringing about the city's fall by starvation rather than through mounting a costly assault.

A further important reason for their action was the imminently expected arrival in the area of several thousand battle-hardened veterans from the English forces in Ireland. The 'cessation' or truce reached between the King's lord deputy in Ireland, the earl of Ormonde and the Irish Confederates, had released these troops for the King to use in England. It was obvious that, faced by Parliamentarian naval superiority, the Leinster Army based around Dublin would attempt the perilous crossing of the Irish Sea at its shortest point, and disembark in the North Wales and Chester areas. The local Parliamentarian

24. Hawarden Castle. As a still substantially intact medieval fortress, Hawarden was an important link in the outer circle of Chester's defences, and in securing its communications with North Wales.

forces had only a short time in which to reach a decision before the balance of power in the area tilted against them.

For the present, however, Brereton and Myddleton were only faced by small and ill-trained local Royalist levies. They attacked the fortified bridge over the Dee at Holt, and after a brief struggle routed its unenthusiastic defenders. At one stroke the Parliamentarians had effectively destroyed Royalist resistance in north-east Wales. Although Holt Castle, under its resolute governor, Lieutenant-Colonel John Robinson, continued to bid defiance, Wrexham 'verie commodious to hinder all the passages to Chester' fell the same day, possibly by treachery.[2]

The local Royalist militia disbanded itself without a fight and, unopposed on the Welsh side of the Dee, Brereton sent detachments of troops to blockade Chester on its English side, establishing themselves at Tarvin and in Wirral, 'so as I hope through God's mercie we may be able to give a good account thereof if care may be taken that the King's forces may not fall downe upon us to oppresse and swallow us up.'[3]

On Saturday 11 November Brereton and Myddleton had another success when they appeared before Hawarden Castle. The Royalist outpost was unprovisioned and possibly in a poor state of repair, and its governor, Colonel Thomas Ravenscroft, promptly surrendered, leading to unproven allegations of treachery.

Whilst his troops occupied themselves with foraging, and wrecking the churches in the places where they were quartered, Brereton summoned Chester to surrender. The deputy governor, Sir Abraham Shipman, responded uncompromisingly that if Sir William wanted the city, he must 'win and wear it'.[4]

But the sudden Parliamentarian success had caused considerable alarm in Chester, where, symptomatic of the paranoia which the series of reverses were causing among the local Royalist leadership, it was blamed by Orlando Bridgeman on 'abominable treachery or cowardice or both.' Morale was not improved when, on 16 November, Shipman gave orders to a tough, and non-local, veteran of the Irish wars, Colonel John Marrow, who commanded a regiment of horse, to burn 'unknown to the Mayor' the Handbridge suburb, 'that the rebels might not shelter there'. Next day Bache and Flookersbrook Halls were also burnt.[5]

The Chester citizens were always understandably reluctant to witness the destruction of their property, and are unlikely to have been reconciled to it by a statement that:

> The military commanders and aldermen of Chester have no purpose of destroying the fortified suburbs of Chester, but on the contrary will with their lives preserve them from violence, this proclamation being issued to discredit certain seditious reports arising out of the recent demolition of the fortified suburb of Handbridge (at the advice of Sir Abraham Shipman, Deputy Governor of the said city) lest it should be occupied by the rebels.[6]

The Royalist cause in Chester was under serious threat, but rescue was at hand.

Ever since the Cessation, Ormonde had been preparing to despatch units of the Leinster Army, but he faced a number of problems. Until seven ships arrived from Royalist-held Bristol, no transport was available. The troops were in rags, ill-fed and unpaid, so that Ormonde, who had well-founded fears concerning the loyalty of some of his officers, was concerned that the men would mutiny or desert once they reached England, and warned:

> if the case be such, that plentifull provision cannot be instantly readie, it is absolutely needful that a competent strength of horse and foot, of whose affections you are confident, should be in redinesse by force to keepe the common soldier in awe; and whatever provision is made for them this will not be amiss...[7]

Bridgeman, in co-operation with John Williams, Archbishop of York, based at Conway, and other Welsh Royalist leaders, had taken charge of preparations to receive the forces from Ireland, and to meet their most urgent needs. Suitably reassured about their reception, Ormonde despatched the first wave, which disembarked at Mostyn in Flintshire on 21 November. They consisted of about 1,500 foot together with two companies of firelocks and a few horse.[8]

Brereton's deceptively complete hold on north-east Wales promptly collapsed. Any hope of engaging the invaders (many of whom were in fact Welshmen from the same locality) dissolved when the Lancashire Parliamentarian troops, citing fear of an attack on Liverpool, went home. An attempt to persuade the 'Irish' troops to defect received 'a short and flat answer', and Brereton beat a hasty retreat back over the Dee into Cheshire, leaving a small garrison to hold Hawarden Castle.

The news of the series of defeats suffered by the Royalist commander on the Welsh Marches, Arthur, Lord Capel, together with Ormonde's warnings about the reliability of the troops from Ireland had made the King decide to send to the area three weak regiments from Lancashire which had been serving with the Oxford Army, together with the regiment of horse of John, 1st Baron Byron of Rochdale, who was to take overall command of the force. Byron set off immediately, and by 30 November was at Shrewsbury with 1,000 horse and 300 foot.

25. John Williams, Archbishop of York (1582–1650). After a stormy pre-war political career, Williams retired to Conway on the outbreak of war, and became a vociferous spokesman for Welsh interests. He came into increasing conflict with the Royalist leadership as a result, and was eventually expelled from Conway by Sir John Owen, and sided with Parliament in the closing stages of the war.

26. John, Lord Byron (c.1600–1652). The eldest of seven brothers who served with the Royalist forces, Byron probably had some pre-war military experience, and had been lieutenant-governor of the Tower of London. A prickly, ambitious but generally competent – if unlucky – commander.

John, Lord Byron was to play a leading role in Royalist operations in and around Chester for the remainder of the war, and it was due to him, more than any other single individual, that such a long and determined resistance was maintained.

The Byron family, of Newstead Abbey, Nottinghamshire, owed their wealth to coal mining interests in that county and in Lancashire. Sir John (as he then was) had been heavily in debt at the outbreak of the war, and it was partly in the hope of retrieving their fortunes from a grateful monarch that the Byrons became such committed Royalists. Sir Nicholas was John's uncle, and John also had six brothers who fought for the Royalist cause.

John Byron was born in about 1603, and was an MP under King James I and Charles I, serving as sheriff of Nottinghamshire in 1634. Like many of his contemporaries, Byron evidently gained some military experience on the Continent and in the Scots War of 1640. In 1641 he was lieutenant-governor of the Tower of London, and regarded by Parliament as a dangerous opponent. On the outbreak of war Byron was given command of the first regiment of horse to be raised for the Royalist field army.

Described by the Earl of Clarendon as: 'As a person of a very ancient family, an honourable extraction, good fortune, and as unblemished a reputation as any gentleman of England', Byron was destined to have a somewhat chequered military career, but plainly he regarded himself as first and foremost a man of war: 'A soldier [and very proud and prickly about it as his correspondence shows] anxious to preserve… his own amour proper'. Another opinion holds him to have been 'Proud, ambitious and heavy-handed… It may be that he was stupid as well.' This latter view is, however, unfair. As a cavalry commander Byron had won a succession of victories, at Burford, Roundway Down and Newbury, and his subsequent defeats in the field, at Nantwich, Marston Moor and Montgomery, may be held to have been as much the result of bad luck as caused by incompetence. During the long months of his defence of Chester, Byron would display determination and resourcefulness, and would show concern for the welfare of his troops, though not always for the civilians caught up in the war.[9]

On arrival at Chester, Byron, with the title 'Field Marshal General of North Wales and those Parts', took command of all Royalist forces in the region, including the troops from Ireland. This was not, as sometimes suggested, the product of a dubious intrigue on his part to supplant Capel, but had been authorised prior to his departure from Oxford. For the moment, Byron was to take command pending the anticipated arrival of Ormonde himself.

Meanwhile the first of the troops from Ireland had reached Chester. They did not create a favourable impression as they marched through the city streets, 'faint, weary, and out of clothing.' The mayor:

> sent through all the wards to get apparel of the citizens, who gave freely, some whole sutes, some two, some doublets, others breeches, others shirts, shoes, stockings and hatts, to the apparelling of about 300.[10]

Orlando Bridgeman, meanwhile, was making more organised efforts throughout North Wales, by which money, shoes, stockings, and a large amount of cloth, some of it green, was obtained to be made into suits for the remainder. Enough was also provided to equip the second wave of Ormonde's troops, the foot regiments of Robert Byron (brother to John) and Henry Warren, 1,300 strong, when they arrived from Dublin early in December.

On 1 December, still apparently inspired by relief at their deliverance, the civic authorities agreed that 300 of the Chester Trained Band should join the companies of Gamull's foot of Captains Thropp and Morgan to assist in the reduction of Hawarden Castle, despite the previous undertaking that they should serve only in the defence of Chester itself. The Parliamentarian garrison, threatened with no quarter, and without hope of relief, surrendered on 4 December.

Chester's enthusiasm for its saviours was now wearing thin. There had been cases of looting and cattle stealing, and of soldiers selling the clothing which they

27. The propaganda view. The looting habits of soldiers were a frequent subject of seventeenth-century propaganda. The troops from Ireland were in fact probably no worse in this respect than many others, but their behaviour seriously upset the citizens of Chester.

had been given in order to obtain money for drink. Though the troops tended to be described, both at the time and later, as 'Irish', the majority actually came from North Wales and its borders, and will have been no strangers to Chester. But, probably originally recruited from the more disreputable elements of the community, they had been hardened and embittered by war and hard usage, and proved uneasy neighbours for the local population. On 1 December, in evident desperation, the Chester assembly voted that £100 of the city plate should be delivered to the Royalist commanders on condition 'that the souldiers be removed forth of this Cittie to quarters elsewhere by Monday next.'[11]

There had been some uncertainty about the best way to employ the forces from Ireland. One possibility, quickly discounted, had been for them to march south to join the King. Another was for them to reinforce the Marquis of Newcastle's Northern Royalists in meeting the imminently expected invasion by Parliament's Scots allies. This probably remained the long-term aim, but it was necessary first to consolidate Royalist control of the north–west by clearing Parliamentarian garrisons in Cheshire and taking Liverpool. It was quite unusual for an army to embark on such a full-scale operation in the depths of winter, and only the urgent need to deal with the local situation before the Scots could intervene made the Royalists undertake such action.

On 12 December Byron led his combined army of about 1,000 horse and 4,000 foot out of Chester on the first stage of his operations. This began well, when, next day, the fiery captain of firelocks Thomas Sandford led eight of his company up the supposedly unscaleable north-west face of Beeston Crag and seized the castle from its Parliamentarian garrison without a shot being fired. The governor, Captain Thomas Steele, an inexperienced soldier, was unwise enough to entertain Sandford to dinner after the surrender, and as a result would later be shot for treachery in Nantwich.[12]

With Chester's outer circle of defences once more entirely in Royalist hands, Byron's forces gradually closed in around Nantwich, the last major Parliamentarian garrison in Cheshire. The Royalists mounted a ruthless campaign. On Christmas Eve some of Byron's troops attacked Bartholmley Church, according to contradictory contemporary accounts apparently held as a garrison by a party of armed civilians led by a local schoolmaster. After they were thought to have surrendered, a shot was fired, and the defenders were smoked out of the church and summarily executed. Such incidents are common enough in the heat of battle, but it provided ready propaganda for the Parliamentarians, particularly as the Royalists regarded their actions as justified by the rules of war. A Parliamentarian newspaper published a letter, allegedly written by Byron, stating:

> The Rebels possessed themselves of a Church at Bartholmley, but wee presently beat them forth of it, and put them all to the sword, which I find to be the best way to proceed with their kind of people, for mercy to them is cruelty.

Whether or not the Royalist commander actually wrote these words, he was henceforth known in Parliamentarian propaganda sheets as 'the Bloody Bragadochio Byron'.[13]

Brereton had meanwhile been attempting to muster a force, including Lancashire troops, to relieve Nantwich, but on 26 December they encountered Byron's forces at Middlewich, and suffered a severe defeat. Brereton fell back on Manchester, and, as Byron began a close siege of Nantwich, appealed urgently to the Parliamentarian authorities at Westminster for assistance.

The only troops available were about 1,500 Yorkshire horse and dragoons under Sir Thomas Fairfax, who were wintering in Lincolnshire. Unpaid and poorly equipped, Fairfax's men were hardly fit for active operations, but, obedient to orders, Fairfax set off north-westwards, picking up reinforcements in the Midlands. However Byron was aware of his approach, and on 13 January his cavalry led by John Marrow beat up Fairfax's troops in their quarters at Ashton-under-Lyne.

28. Sir Thomas Fairfax (1612–72). As commander of the New Model Army in the
latter stages of the war, Fairfax would play a major role in Parliament's victory.
In early 1644 he was still relatively unknown, acting as second in command to
his father in the Army of the Northern Association.

This Royalist success was partly offset on 14 January when an ammunition
convoy on its way through the Midlands to join Byron was captured at
Ellesmere in Shropshire. Among the prisoners was Sir Nicholas Byron, on his
way back to resume his post as governor of Chester, this time directly answer-
able to the King instead of to the assembly. Lord Byron remained confident of
victory, however, telling Prince Rupert that he hoped shortly to give him a
good account of Nantwich, 'without which all we have done in this countrie
is nothing.'[14]

On 18 January 1644 the Royalists launched a full-scale assault on the little
market town. After furious fighting, which left the barricaded entrances to the
Parliamentarian stronghold piled with dead, the attack was repulsed. Among
several hundred Royalist fatalities was the bombastic Captain Thomas Sandford.

But the garrison had gained only a temporary respite; probably more
concerned by the expenditure of his limited supply of ammunition than by his
casualties, Byron, his troops surrounding Nantwich on both banks of the River
Weaver, remained optimistic of success within a short time.

Fairfax meanwhile had reached Manchester, where he scraped together a
force of horse and foot and on 21 January set off through deep snow to the
relief of Nantwich. Three days later he was approaching the town, and Byron,

who was reluctant to lift the siege until the last possible moment, in order to prevent the garrison from foraging, prepared for battle the next day. He hoped to meet Fairfax several miles to the west of Nantwich, but his plans were disrupted by a sudden thaw during the night, which caused the level of the River Weaver to rise sharply, sweeping away the pontoon bridge, and temporarily splitting the Royalist army.

The battle of Nantwich fought the following day was a confusing affair, in which neither of the opposing commanders displayed particular skill. A hard-fought action, it came close to being a Royalist victory, but their probable shortage of ammunition together with the possible defection of some of the troops from Ireland tipped the scales against the Royalists. An attack on their rear by the Nantwich garrison completed Byron's defeat, and resulted in the surrender of most of his foot.[15]

Byron himself, with his horse and about 1,000 foot, withdrew to Chester. Though his campaign had ended in disaster, Chester, partly because of the recovery of Beeston Castle, was in no immediate danger. But the presence in the city of Byron and the remnants of his veterans was the beginning of a grimmer phase of the war for the citizens of Chester. From now onwards, control of their lives would pass increasingly into the hands of the military, with far-reaching consequences.

The return of the soldiers from Ireland, fewer in numbers, but uglier in mood and including a number of wounded requiring care, was an unpleasant consequence of the defeat at Nantwich. The outcome was a series of complaints to the military leadership regarding a wide range of festering griev-ances. They included the grant of free quarters, by which troops were billeted on a citizen and maintained at his expense, the apparent failure of the wounded to return to duty, and brawling by armed soldiers in Chester's streets. Their womenfolk and children were accused of various disorders, there were allega-tions of robbery, while the troops from Ireland were accused of not attending church on Sundays! To these complaints were added more long-standing disputes over the demolition of property in the suburbs, the cost of main-taining the defences, and the use of Chester troops beyond the city limits.[16]

Byron admitted that discipline among his men was poor, and took stern measures against them, as references show:

1643 [1644], February.
    An Irish soldier was hanged on the gibbet for killing his fellow soldier desperately in Ran. Ashbrook's house, Taylor, in Eastgate St.

1643 [1644], March 17th

Another soldier was hanged for making a mutiny on Saboth day; about the same time another soldier was hanged at two mills of the heath for the like offence.[17]

Early in February two more foot regiments from Ireland, those of Henry Tillier and Robert Broughton, arrived, but Byron, with the resources of the Chester area already over-stretched, sent them on to Shrewsbury. Here Prince Rupert had taken command of Royalist forces in North Wales and its borders, in place of Ormonde, whose presence was needed in Ireland. Byron warned the prince on 21 February that they expected the same treatment as previous arrivals:

a month's entertainment; for every common soldier half a crown, a suit of clothes, shoes and stockings. Since their coming the officers have had only their month's pay, but the men have had free quarters and 12d a week, which is more than they ever had in Ireland.

If their needs were not met, Byron feared that the troops would mutiny, to which 'they are inclined as any soldiers in the world.'[18]

Meanwhile the capture of Sir Nicholas Byron had sparked off problems regarding his replacement as governor of Chester. The civilian leadership in Chester saw an opportunity to obtain the position for one of their own. Francis Gamull, currently serving in the Royalist Parliament in Oxford, pressed his own claims to the King. He was already concerned about reported neglect of the needs of his own regiment at Chester, writing on 13 February to the mayor urging the continued collection of assessments to pay his men, 'because money best stoppeth all discontented mens' mouths.' He was concerned about the condition of his regiment, 'which when I was at Chester was full of loyalty, duty and diligence', but was now displaying 'carelessnesse'. Gamull had received reports that some of his men were to be used to fill out Byron's depleted units from Ireland. This must have been of particular concern to the 'Brethren', threatening as it did to weaken the main instrument of their control in Chester. But his letter was also the opening shot in a campaign by Gamull to be appointed governor.[19]

The King, in typically unassertive fashion, did not discourage Gamull in his desires, writing to Prince Rupert that if he decided to appoint Gamull as governor 'we shall very well approve of your choice.' However a letter of 13 February from his secretary of state, Lord George Digby, was less enthusiastic.

His Majesty hath written to you in favour of one Colonel Gamel, of Chester, a person very well deserving of his Majesty's service; and his Majesty doth earnestly recommend him to your care and favour in point of his regiment; but for the government of Chester, your Highness will easily believe that his Majesty is induced to give him that recommendation only for his satisfaction's sake.[20]

As a civilian, Gamull's appointment would have been contrary to Rupert's policy of placing key positions in the hands of professional soldiers. He had already replaced the civilian governor of Shrewsbury, and it is highly unlikely that he would have favoured a reversal of this process at Chester. In any case, the prospect of Gamull's appointment was meeting with opposition from influential sources at Chester. The county commissioners of array and the Cheshire Royalist gentry were alarmed at the prospect of an extension of the power of Chester's civil authorities. Byron strongly supported their opposition, writing to Rupert on 21 February:

Since I writt last night to yr Highness, there is a report spread in this towne that gives greate discontent to all well-affected people, which is that at the instance of the Parliament at Oxford, the Kinge hath recommended to yr Highness Alderman Gamull, who hath a regiment of foot heere, to bee governor of this citty. I thought his Majesty had already had sufficient experience of Corporations not to intrust them with the command of a place of such importance as this is, and therefore it is persuaded much against his own judgement, and since it is referred to yr Highness, I hope you will bee pleased to make a stopp of it, the consequence of it being so dangerous, that if this bee admitted of, the like will be attempted in all the corporations in England that are under his Majestie's obedience, and if one obtaine it, the rest will never be satisfied, till they have Governors of their owne...[21]

Soon afterwards Prince Rupert, as captain-general of Wales and the Marches, set off on a tour of key positions in his command. Chester was high on his agenda, particularly perhaps because of the dissension there. Rupert arrived in the city on 11 March, greeted ceremonially with the ringing of church bells, and streets lined with troops and citizens, the aldermen in their mulberry coloured robes and JPs in scarlet. He was met by Lord Byron and his officers, who escorted him to the High Cross, where the mayor, Randle Holme, despite being 'ill of a payne in the legg' delivered a speech of welcome,

29. Prince Rupert (1619–82). Rupert owed his appointment as general of horse more to his being the King's nephew than as a result of any proven military ability. He turned out to be a highly capable cavalry commander and administrator, though his abrasive personality, youth and limited experience rendered him less suited for higher command.

somewhat diluted by a recital of the list of complaints described earlier. The prince supposedly took the lecture 'very kindly', though significantly offered no concessions, with the result that the aldermen and JPs refused to meet the prince next morning, after he had spent the night at the Watergate Street home of leading merchant John Aldersley. Holme's bad leg had suffered a diplomatic relapse during the night, so that he also failed to appear.

In the event this boycott was probably an ill-considered response by the Brethren. The outcome was that Byron and the military had the undisputed ear of the prince that morning as he toured Chester's defences. Probably devised by Rupert's engineer, Bernard de Gomme, a number of improvements were ordered. They included:

The enlarging the ditches of the works both in breadth and depth, raised the mud walls, which before were but breast high to that height a man might walk within the works and not be seen from without, cut the rock without the Northgate beyond Dutton's Turnpike in a great Trench [the modern Rock Lane], made several new mounts about Cowlane, cutt off part of the old Trenches and made new by the advice of the Prince's engineers...[22]

The original salient of outworks which had extended to Flookersbrook was abandoned. The new mounts were Reeds Mount, Phoenix Tower Mount, Jousting Croft Mount and Cock Pit Mount, all much more formidable and professionally designed than the earlier defences.[23]

In a significant move for the future of Royalist Chester, Rupert gave 'lord Byron directions for the further strengthening and management of the place.'[24] The civilian leadership of Chester had been sidelined, and there would be no further mention of Gamull's appointment as governor. For the present Sir Abraham Shipman remained as deputy, but it was clearly the prince's intention that henceforward control should be in the hands of the military.

The next few weeks saw a partial Royalist recovery along the Welsh Border. Sir Thomas Fairfax had been called away to pursue the siege of Lathom House in Lancashire, and Brereton was also absent. Byron's depleted regiments had been filled out by new conscripts and exchanged prisoners, together with the first contingent of his own regiment of foot, raised in part in Dublin from 'native' Irish. Thus strengthened, in April Byron carried out some successful minor operations against Parliamentarian garrisons in nearby Maelor.

Meanwhile Prince Rupert, his reputation and share of limited Royalist resources boosted by his recent relief of Newark (21 March), turned his attention towards Lancashire. Once he had relieved Lathom House, and more importantly, cleared communications with Ireland by taking the key port of Liverpool, he would cross the Pennines to support the Marquis of Newcastle against the Scots.

The deteriorating situation in the north forced the Royalists to move more quickly than Byron, at least, would have liked, fearing as he did the collapse of insecure Royalist control of the Marches in the event of Rupert suffering a reverse. For, as well as ruthlessly conscripting new levies, the prince, he felt with some justice, had stripped the Royalist garrisons to a dangerous degree. Chester played its part in these preparations. Byron and most of his troops were drawn off to join the field army, which by mid-May was ready to march.[25]

In Chester itself, Sir Abraham Shipman was transferred to be governor of Oswestry. In his place came one of Prince Rupert's closest followers, his general of ordnance, Sergeant-Major-General William Legge.

'Honest Will Legge' as the prince called him, born in about 1609, was a typical professional soldier. He had served with the Dutch and Swedes, been governor of Hull, and during the Civil War had fought with competence if no great flair in several actions. Noted as being 'a very punctual and steady observer of the orders he received, but no contriver of them', Legge was an unimaginative 'safe pair of hands'. He could be relied upon to carry out

Rupert's wishes with regard to the military administration of Chester, but would prove a highly unpopular governor with its citizens.[26]

Legge took over on 19 May, the same day that Byron and his forces joined Rupert at Knutsford on the first stage of his Lancashire campaign. Despite his uncompromising approach towards civilians, Rupert had made some attempt to smooth Chester's ruffled civic feathers. Gamull, no doubt as a sop for his rejection as governor, had been made a baronet. In April when impressment had been introduced to build up Rupert's army, the citizens of Chester, provided they enlisted in Gamull's regiment, had been exempted, and Sir Francis himself was now appointed deputy governor under Legge, though with circumscribed powers. Writing to the assembly, Rupert described Legge as:

> A Person every way Qualified for soe Great and Important a Trust… you shall find him no less industrious to Promote your Service, both of that Place, and of your Persons and fortune…[27]

The prince was careful to ensure that real control was firmly in the hands of the military, however. Affairs were to be directed by a quorum of at least four officers and local Royal officials. The only representative of the Chester civil authorities named was the mayor, and for any decisions to be valid, the governor or his deputy had to be present. In an early sign of a harder line, three days after Legge's appointment an abrupt order was delivered to the Brethren, requiring

30. William Legge (1609?–70). A professional soldier, Legge became a close supporter and friend of Prince Rupert. An unimaginative though reliable officer, Legge was unpopular in Chester.

that the suburb of Handbridge, whose inhabitants had so far dragged their feet over orders for its demolition, should 'be forthwith levelled to the ground'.[28]

Even in the midst of his victorious operations in Lancashire, Rupert kept an eye on affairs in Chester. On 11 June from newly captured Liverpool he wrote to the mayor and aldermen:

> Strictly to charge and command you to make and settle a rate and assessment on all and over the Inhabitants of your City and the Suburbs thereof for the maintainance and pay of the Souldiers of the Regiment of the said City, and the officers of the same, and likewise of the officers and mynesters of and belonging to the Garrison of the said Citty.[29]

The backbone of the garrison continued to be Gamull's regiment, along with various units from Lord Capel's old command. Among these was the regiment of horse commanded by Colonel John Marrow, which by its raiding operations around Chester soon earned for its commander the nickname among his opponents of 'a second Nimrod'. However Marrow failed on 3 July in an attempt to recover Oswestry, lost a few days earlier in fulfilment of Byron's fears. The failure to regain the town severed direct communications between Chester and Shrewsbury.

Meanwhile the citizens of Chester had been following reports of Rupert's progress with keen attention. On 22 May,

> beinge Tuesday, was a general fast in the great Church kept for the prosperity of Prince Rupert's army being advanced towards Cheshire and thence to Lancaster. 6 June, being Thursday, was a Thanksgiving Sermon made to God in St Werburgh's for this victory of Prince Rupert [the capture of Bolton on 28 May]. The bells range and bonfires were made at almost every dore for joy of his Highness good successe.[30]

However at the same time there was considerable discontent in Chester, as in other areas under Royalist control, concerning the King's action in imposing an excise duty on the sale of various basic commodities.

> So the mayor caused all councillors of every ward… to bring all citizens inhabitants and others with their armes to the Roodee – the soldiers keeping strict watch in mean season at the outworks. The Royalists came willingly, the suspected malignants came creeping to shew themselves, more for fear than love. The whole citizens set on by the said

malignants called on the mayor much to desist further prosecution of the said excise – he promised to represent their desires. At same time, came a runner that Sir W. Brereton and his forces were coming again and nigh the town which caused each man with all expedition to his ward and guard, but the alarm proved false.[31]

The report may have been sent deliberately in order to disperse the irate citizens, among whom feelings continued to run high, as they would demonstrate in the mayoral elections of October.

On 2 July Prince Rupert suffered a crushing defeat at Marston Moor in Yorkshire. Once again Chester's streets were filled with the debris of a defeated army when Rupert on 25 July made his headquarters in the city and began feverish efforts to rebuild his forces.

He was thought by Sir William Brereton to have about 5,000 horse with him, mostly quartered on the Welsh side of the Dee, while 800 horse under Marrow occupied a forward position at Tarvin. Royalist losses at Marston Moor had fallen particularly heavily on the foot, but not least among the casualties had been Rupert's reputation for invincibility, and his new levies deserted almost as quickly as they were raised.

Hopes of retaining a Royalist foothold in Lancashire, which would have at least eased pressure on Chester, were dashed on 21 August, when Byron's forces were defeated at Ormskirk and forced to fall back into Cheshire. Rupert may already have decided to transfer his headquarters to Bristol even before the Royalists suffered yet another reverse.

On 21 August John Marrow's career came to an abrupt end. He had continued his raiding throughout the summer, and Brereton and Myddleton were anxious to curb this major irritant. Capturing some of Marrow's scouts they learnt that the Royalists were apparently quartered at Tarvin taking few precautions against attack. Marrow was possibly taken by surprise, and routed. Part of his regiment was trapped in Tarvin Church and forced to surrender. Others, including Marrow himself, fled towards Chester, pursued by some of Brereton's regiment of horse under Major Jerome Zankey. During the chase Marrow was shot and mortally wounded by a musketeer concealed in a hedge. Though his regiment would take the field again under his successor, Robert Werden, Marrow's death was a serious blow to the Chester Royalists.

Fortune continued to run against the King's cause in Cheshire. After thoroughly plundering the countryside around Chester, Sir Marmaduke Langdale and 3,000 northern horse, the remains of the army of the Marquis of Newcastle, suffered a serious mauling from Brereton's cavalry on 26 August at Malpas.[32]

An even more serious defeat was inflicted on the Royalists in September. His successes during August had given Brereton control of all of Cheshire apart from Wirral, Beeston Castle and the immediate vicinity of Chester, and opened the way for a thrust into mid-Wales. On 3 September Parliamentarian forces under Sir Thomas Myddleton and Colonel Thomas Mytton, commanding in Shropshire, bloodlessly occupied Montgomery Castle, severing direct communications between Shrewsbury and mid-Wales.

Byron reacted strongly, mustering all available troops from Chester and Shrewsbury in an attempt to retake Montgomery. However on 18 September, in a hard-fought action, the excellent Cheshire Parliamentarian foot proved a match for the remnants of the troops from Ireland and Royalist cavalry who had not recovered from their recent defeats at Marston Moor and Ormskirk. The last of the army from Ireland was effectively destroyed, and Byron left incapable of challenging the enemy in open battle.[33]

Pressure on Chester was increasing steadily. Though a new threat from Myddleton to North Wales receded after the Parliamentarian commander was checked on 19 October by the garrison of Ruthin Castle, the danger to Chester was growing. Sir John Meldrum had now laid close siege to Sir Robert Byron's garrison at Liverpool, freeing the bulk of the Lancashire Parliamentarian forces for other operations. In September they crossed the Mersey into Wirral, and at Birkenhead captured 'a great piece of Ordnance' which had been sent from Chester to cover the mouth of the Mersey, and took sixty prisoners.[34]

On 26 October the garrison of Beeston Castle suffered a reverse at Tilston Heath during a sortie against Parliamentarian cattle raiders from Nantwich, and on 16 November Brereton's forces began a blockade of the castle.

Within Chester, growing discontent at the new excise, and perhaps the birth of a desire not to be too irrevocably bound to what might prove to be the losing side, caused the citizens to reject Sir Francis Gamull in the mayoral elections. Instead they chose Alderman Charles Walley. Byron was later to denounce Walley for lack of support during the siege, and, as we shall see later, he does seem to have played an equivocal role in its later stages. But in 1642 he had been closely associated with the inner circle of the Brethren who had secured the city for the Royalists, and as yet he was still active in the King's cause. However Walley was not in the same ultra-Royalist league as Byron and Gamull, and his election was evidence of growing caution within Chester.

Randle Holme, the retiring mayor, handed over office with a speech reflecting the thoughts of many of Chester's citizens:

31. Montgomery Castle. An eighteenth-century engraving showing this key fortress after its slighting by Parliament at the end of the war.

Gentle, I am glad of this yeare's period that I come to give you of the commons thanks for your approbation, and you of the bench thanks for your confirmation of this great honour on me to be your Chief magistrate being farre unworthy thereof; which honour brought a great burden with it in respect of the tymes troublesomeness; for what my predecessors only with the finger touched I have heavily felt, but by God's mercy have run through the same, although with many an aking heart; for to see our antient plate diminished, our benefactors' money exhausted, the cittizens estates impoverished, our suburbs fired and cittizens oppressed (the necessity of the tymes requiring it and I much greeved I could not remedy it) only our comfort was, it was for a good Kinge and in a good cause: and though in all things I could not do what I would, yet I have done what I promised in performance of my loyalty and preservation of this city for his Majesty, and I hope my successor will do the same to whom I leave the city and privileges in good order; the stone and mud walls in good condition far better than I found them; and as a dying man I bequeath my staffe, place and authority to you and you to God, and God give you much joy and peace therein to God's glory, the King's honour and tranquillity of the citty, and so I take my leave.[35]

But for Holme's successor and the citizens of Chester, the great time of trial was about to begin.

4

THE LEAGUER BEGINS:
NOVEMBER 1644–MAY 1645

Throughout the summer, Royalist Chester had been making preparations to meet a renewed attack. In July the assembly had ordered assessments for repairs to the mud walls and their gates, and cleaning the ditch by the Eastgate, and in September a further assessment of £100 a week was levied to maintain the garrison.[1]

Even after the defeat at Montgomery, there was no great shortage of manpower. The remnants of Byron's field army were now largely confined to the city or the Welsh side of the Dee, and so were added to the strength of the garrison. The troops available included Byron and Gamull's regiments of foot, respectively at least 300 and 600 strong. There were also the 300 men of Sir Roger Mostyn's regiment from Flintshire and Denbighshire, and the remnants of several of the English regiments from Ireland. Also available was Prince Rupert's regiment of 'Bluecoats', under Colonel John Russell, being rebuilt with new recruits after its heavy losses at Marston Moor. In total there were probably 2,500–3,000 foot in Chester at this time, together with Lord Byron's, Robert Werden's, Marcus Trevor's and Roger Whitley's regiments of horse, about 1,000 troopers in all.[2]

But although manpower may not have been a pressing problem, personality clashes were. Relations between Byron and Legge (still governor of Chester) seem to have steadily deteriorated. In part this was the inevitable result of circumstances. Byron's troops were competing for resources with the garrison units, and though Byron also had responsibility for the currently largely inactive North Wales theatre of operations, his concentration was increasingly

1. The fourteenth-century Abbey Gateway, main entrance to Abbey Square, where were situated the residences of the Bishop of Chester and other leading clergy.

2. View eastwards along the northern section of the city walls. Note the solid rock on which the foundations of the walls at this point stand. The canal occupies the approximate line of the dry Fosse or ditch of the time of the siege.

3. The Dee Bridge, looking south westwards towards Handbridge. Other than slight widening, the bridge remains largely unaltered from the time of the siege. The site of the fortified gatehouse which stood at the southern end of the bridge is indicated by the larger buttress at that end.

4. The Bridge Street house of the Cowper family, leading Chester Royalists. Like many contemporary buildings in the city, the house was partially rebuilt in later years.

5. The 'Old King's Head', Lower Bridge Street. Originally a sixteenth- or seventeenth-century building which was the residence of Randle Holme during the siege.

6. View from the Welsh side of the Dee looking from the approximate line of the Parliamentarian siegeworks in the later stages of the Leaguer. Note the weir (centre), the Dee Bridge and Bridgegate. The County Hall (left background) occupies part of the site of the castle.

7. Detail of the exterior of 'God's Providence House'. The inscription is said to refer to the residents being spared in an outbreak of the plague.

8. The 'Bear and Billet' (Lower Bridge Street) is dated 1664, and, a former town house of the Earls of Shrewsbury, is an example of the extensive rebuilding which took place as Chester regained its prosperity after the siege.

9. The High Cross. Demolished by the Parliamentarians after the siege, the remains of the cross were buried nearby and subsequently re-erected on their present site. To the right is St Peter's Church, along the southern front of which stood the Pentice.

10. The memorial window to Gamull's regiment in Farndon Church, erected c.1660 by Captain William Barnston, a former officer of the regiment (and ironically briefly arrested for suspected treachery following the loss of the Chester suburbs in September 1645). Some of the panels are intended to depict individual officers of the regiment (including Sir Francis Gamull in the centre panel outside the tent), though it is unclear how far these are accurate portraits. Dress and equipment of the soldiers is apparently based on mid-seventeenth century French style, and is not necessarily an accurate guide to the appearance of Gamull's men.

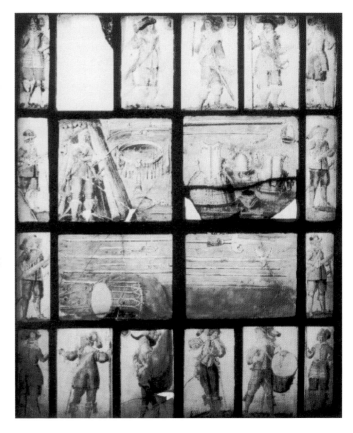

11. Foregate Street, Chester. This was the main route through the eastern suburbs leading out from the Eastgate towards Boughton, Chrisleton and the Parliamentarian advanced headquarters at Tarvin. When the suburbs were surprised in September 1645 Parliamentarian troops advanced rapidly along Foregate Street, almost seizing control of the Eastgate.

12. Women and children accompanied the English troops who came over from Ireland in late 1643 in support of the Royalists. Parliamentarian propaganda claimed that many of the women were 'native Irish', armed with long knives, but in fact they were probably a mixture of English, Irish and Welsh, most of them in established relationships with soldiers.

13. The Kaleyards postern gate seen here was was used by the garrison for an unsuccessful sally after the loss of the suburbs. Note that the walls in this sector, even without the effects of later redevelopment, were significantly lower than elsewhere.

14. The Newgate was replaced by a wider gateway of the same name (on the left) in the twentieth century, and the old gate renamed the Wolfgate. The battlements were a nineteenth-century addition.

15. Site of the Parliamentarian bridge of boats near Dee Lane, seen from the Welsh side of the river.

16. Reconstruction of a Civil War artillery position. Note the breastwork and 'gabions' or earth-filled baskets protecting the gunners. In the right foreground is a linstock, carrying burning match used to fire the cannon.

17. The Phoenix Tower, from which King Charles I watched the closing stages of the battle of Rowton Heath.

18. Site of the breach near the Newgate. The later repairs carried out with a variety of sizes of masonry are clearly visible.

19. Parliamentarian battery position seen from the city walls. In the later stages of the siege a Parliamentarian battery was sited on a bowling green on the southern side of St John's Church, just beyond the group of trees (centre).

20. Barnaby's Tower, a turret at the south-east angle of the city walls, bears the marks of cannon shot fired from the Parliamentarian battery on the bowling green near St John's Church.

21. View from Handbridge, looking across the Dee Bridge with the Bridgegate and Bridge Street in the background. The hydro-electric station (left background) is on the site of some of the Dee Mills.

22. Chester Cathedral. Whilst viewing part of the battle of Rowton Heath from the tower an officer standing beside the King was killed by sniper fire from the steeple of St John's Church.

23. A section of the city walls in the vicinity of the Goblin Tower, showing the steep escarpment which Parliamentarian attackers had to scale.

24. In an effort to reduce the effects of artillery bombardment, the inner sides of the city walls were lined with earth embankments. Traces of these may still remain at Abbey Green in the north-east angle of the walls near King Charles' Tower.

25. View of the gun platform known as Morgan's Mount, on the northern sector of the city walls.

26. View along the city walls westwards towards Pemberton's Parlour (Goblin Tower). The circular tower originally straddled the wall, but, partly because of damage inflicted by Parliamentarian cannon fire, the southern portion was demolished early in the eighteenth century and the remainder converted into an alcove with seats.

27. The New Tower.

28. This view of the section of the city walls near Pemberton's Parlour from the Parliamentarian viewpoint gives an idea of the steep slope which the attackers had to scale.

29. The view along Eastgate Street from the Eastgate demonstrates the relatively small area within the city walls in which the defenders were confined during the closing months of the siege. St Peter's Church whose tower is visible (centre background) was in the centre of the town.

30. Watergate Street. Many of the buildings in this part of the street were destroyed in the Parliamentarian mortar bombardment. Among their replacements was 'God's Providence House' (the half-timbered building, centre). Some of the famous 'Rows' are clearly visible.

31. The sconce built by the garrison and known as Fort Royal probably stood on the higher ground beyond the modern development in this view looking across the Dee from the city walls.

32. Remains in Queen's Meadows of the 'mount' constructed by the Parliamentarians to protect the southern end of the bridge of boats.

32. Musketeer. This soldier has wrapped the lock and muzzle of his musket as protection against bad weather. His clothing shows the effects of prolonged campaigning.

focused on Chester, where Legge theoretically held sway. The two men evidently resented each others' presence, and Legge had lost no opportunity to cast Byron in the main role as culprit for the defeat at Ormskirk in August. On 7 October Byron expressed his frustration in a letter to Prince Rupert:

I supposed that, in Yr Highness absence, the sole command of these countries had beene in mee, as formerly it was, before Yr Highness came into these parts: and that noe orders were to bee obeyed but mine, or sent by any other authority. But I find that there are now independent commissions granted, without any relation at all to mee: in particular, the Governor of Chester hath one of these countryes of Chester, Flint and Denbigh; so that I stand here but for a cipher, onely this advantage I have, to bee liable to the blame of any Errors committed; which is so sadd a condition, that I shall humbly desire Yr Highness, if I bee not worthy of the command I have formerly had, to recall mee from this.

I am confident Yr Highness will doe mee the right to say, I have beene as little guilty of disputes as any man that ever served you, and therefore hope you will not think I complain now, but upon just grounds; neyther doe I at all envy any power Yr Highness hath given

65

Will Legg (who hath ever beene my good frend): but to be exercised in so ample a manner whilst I am present, so much lessens mee in the esteeme of all men here, that I cannot but resent it, humbly submittinge to Yr Highness better consideration.[3]

Legge was, of course, Rupert's man, and Byron's formerly amicable relationship with the prince seems to have deteriorated sharply after Marston Moor, partly because Rupert scapegoated Byron for his defeat there. He also increasingly drew on Byron's resources to rebuild his own forces. Byron reacted by moving closer to the faction headed by Lord George Digby, secretary of state and opponent of Rupert, and to the Earl of Ormonde. At one point in the spring of 1645, angered by Rupert's withdrawal of troops from Chester, he seems to have considered resigning and withdrawing to Ireland. The Royalist commissioners of array and city authorities also disliked Legge, and Byron at some point during the year cemented his relations with the Cheshire gentry by marrying Eleanor, daughter of Lord Kilmorrey.[4]

Archbishop John Williams, observing events from Conway Castle, expressed grave anxiety about the situation in a letter of 30 October to Ormonde:

It is thought that that city is full of disaffected persons, and certain that they do not love their present Governor, as it is also that the enemy knows too well what little accord there is between Legge and the Prince's creatures with that poor Lord who commands, or should command in chief in these parts. A most worthy man, but unfortunately matcht in his Government.[5]

Brereton meanwhile was drawing closer. During October he was operating in Wirral, quartering outposts at Stanney and Great Neston, and fortifying Hooton House. Whilst still not strong enough to begin a regular blockade of Chester, his cavalry launched cattle raids in its vicinity, generally getting the best of the ensuing skirmishes. On 28 October Brereton wrote to the Committee of Both Kingdoms in London, the directing body of the Parliamentarian and Scots war effort:

Our garrison at Tarvin is in good forwardness, and we proceed with all expedition in fortifying Hooton in Wirral. The enemy is raising all the forces possible in Wales, with which they hope to struggle with us until the arrival of the forces expected to come down with the Prince from the King's army, which is not to be doubted is a great part of their care.[6]

Further assisted by the fall of Liverpool on 2 November, Sir William Brereton prepared to concentrate on the great strategic prize of Chester, the last remaining major Royalist garrison in the north-west.

Brereton had gained some military experience during the opening years of the war, though he was clearly a better administrator than field commander, and made a practice of employing professional soldiers in some key positions. Under his command was his horse, led by Colonel Michael Jones, son of the bishop of Killaloe in Ireland, though of Cheshire origin. Jones had gained a reputation in the war against the Irish Confederates before taking a commission under Brereton in 1644. Jones had a high opinion of his own ability, and was frequently impatient with what he saw as his superior's over-cautious approach.[7]

Brereton's major-general of foot was Scottish professional soldier James Lothian, who had served with the Cheshire forces since January 1643, and did much to ensure their success. Unlike Jones, Lothian seems to have been tactful as well as able, and was generally liked by his colleagues.[8]

Brereton's colonels were a mixed bunch, though they included some men of real ability, such as Colonel John Booth, governor of Warrington, and Lieutenant-Colonel Chidley Coote, commanding the Shropshire horse serving with Sir William.

The troops of the Cheshire Army came from a variety of sources. The backbone were the forces raised by the Parliamentarian Cheshire county committee, which formed three main categories. Orginally most had theoretically been volunteers, though coercion had been involved in enlisting many of them. In the summer of 1644 impressment had been authorised for the Parliamentarian forces, and Brereton's ranks included increasing numbers of conscripts. There were also a small number of English troops from Ireland who had switched sides either through desertion or after being taken prisoner, notably at Nantwich.

On occasion the 'regular' forces were supplemented by companies of the county Trained Bands, and infrequently, in times of emergency, by a call-up of some of the militia.

Regiments acted mainly as administrative units, for, given the small-scale nature of much of the fighting the normal tactical unit in Brereton's army was the company of foot or troop of horse. When the need arose these were very effectively formed into 'task forces' made up of men from several regiments. In theory Brereton had about 700 horse and 4,500 foot under his command, but not all were available for active operations, as garrisons, the blockade of Beeston Castle, and general wastage and inefficiency absorbed quite a number.

In order to maintain his blockade of Chester, Brereton was reliant upon assistance from so-called 'auxiliary' troops from outside Cheshire. These varied considerably from time to time both in numbers and effectiveness, and were always liable to withdrawal if their home areas appeared to be under threat, or simply because of disagreements or lack of means to maintain them. Brereton was joined initially by troops from Staffordshire, an area effectively under his own control, and at various times men from Lancashire, Yorkshire, Warwickshire and Shropshire.

Sir William's main day-to-day concern, apart from sifting intelligence reports of enemy intentions, was providing pay and supplies for his troops. The system employed in raising revenue is obscure and apparently chaotic, and references in his correspondence to the problems which it gave Brereton are legion. In general terms, though, Brereton usually managed to provide his Cheshire troops with enough support to prevent them from actually deserting, though he was much less successful so far as his troops from other areas were concerned.[9]

During Brereton's periods of absence from the local scene, usually when he was at Westminster, control was exercised by the County Committee, some of whose members, notably the Booth family, who were presbyterian moderates, resented Brereton on religious and political grounds. The

33. John Booth. Son of Sir George Booth the elder, John was a capable soldier with the Cheshire Parliamentarian forces, though often suspected of pursuing his own agenda. Like his father, Booth became disillusioned with political trends during and after the war, and by 1648 was an active pro-Royalist conspirator.

34. Sir George Booth (the younger, 1622–84). A political and religious opponent of Sir William Brereton, Booth was a dominant figure among the Cheshire Parliamentarians in Sir William's absence. After the war he opposed the rise of the army and the independent faction, and in 1659 headed an abortive pro-Royalist rising in Cheshire.

committee were generally less effective than Sir William in handling operations, though they had the good sense to leave day-to-day matters in the hands of Jones and Lothian.

Brereton's relations with some of his fellow commanders were as fraught as those among the Royalists. His alliance with Sir Thomas Myddleton had always been based upon mutual self-interest, and, as their areas of operations diverged, the point was eventually reached when Myddleton allowed some of his officers to conduct a 'smear' campaign against Sir William in the hope of engineering his removal from command.

The difficulties facing the Cheshire Parliamentarians were immense. Chester was well garrisoned, and its defences had been greatly strengthened since the outbreak of war. The Welsh side of the city was still open for supplies, and, because of the natural obstacles of river and marsh, virtually impossible to completely close off. And it was hardly likely that the Royalist high command would permit a garrison of such great strategic importance to fall lightly into enemy hands.

Early in December, as part of his plan to tighten the blockade of Chester, Brereton established new garrisons at Aldford, Hawarden, Trafford and Upton Hill, within a 3- or 4-mile radius of the city, and early in January 1645 moved still closer by establishing an outpost, under the command of Jones and Lothian, at Chrisleton.

The Royalists struck back with a series of raids, which inflicted a number of casualties. In one operation the garrison of Holt Castle under Sir Richard Lloyd built a bridge of boats and made a night attack on the Parliamentarians holding the Farndon end of Holt Bridge, which 'did some harme.'[10]

On 16 January Brereton admitted to the Committee of Both Kingdoms:

> the garrison of Chester have been lately more active than formerly, and have fallen upon some of our quarters and taken twenty or thirty men besides horses at several times, which we have not been able to retaliate because none of them are quartered on this side the Dee except those within the walls of Chester and Beeston Castle.[11]

However Beeston Castle was becoming increasingly short of provisions, and concern over this and the new Parliamentarian outpost at Chrisleton caused the Royalists on 18 January to attempt their most ambitious operation so far.

Byron and Legge mustered about 600 horse and 800 foot for an attack with two planned stages. Firstly they would attack the outpost at Chrisleton 'whiles they were at dinner', burn the village and then press on and relieve Beeston.

But perhaps because of friction between Byron and Legge or as a result of the reluctance of the city regiment to take part, the operation was misman-aged from the outset. There was considerable delay in the expedition setting out, marching along Foregate Street and leaving the outworks at Boughton Turnpike. The Parliamentarians at Chrisleton received ample warning of the enemy approach, and drew out a force including about 700 foot to meet them.

The Royalists, after a dilatory advance 'rather for a May show than a warlike procession' were considerably strung out, with the vanguard of about 300 musketeers becoming engaged whilst their main body was still leaving the outworks. The Royalist vanguard attempted to occupy a holding position in the hedgerows along the lane between Boughton and Chrisleton until their main force could join them, but Jones and Major Jerome Zankey at the head of their horse charged them. Royalist soldiers, many of them raw recruits, were so 'terrified' that 'many of them cast down their Armes'. Particularly to blame, according to Randle Holme, was Prince Rupert's regiment: 'the Blucoats rann ere they shott, and flange way their drummes, wheeling towards the waterside [the Dee] to save themselves'. Jones and Zanckey caught the Royalist horse still attempting to deploy, and drove them back towards the outworks, whilst Lothian's Parliamentarian foot cleared the Royalist musketeers remaining in the hedgerows leading to Boughton.

Before Royalist reinforcements could enter the fight, the Parliamentarians made an orderly withdrawal to Chrisleton, driving along with them some prisoners, 'and whom we could not bring off we cut and slashed miserably, which caused many to supplicate themselves prisoners, that they might escape wounds.'

Royalist casualties in this mismanaged affair were heavy. Though they lost relatively few dead, apart from forty men said to have been drowned in the Dee, large numbers were taken prisoner. The common soldiers captured were claimed to be:

> most of them Chester men, as Shoemakers, Cobblers, Taylors, Barbers and the like… to the great amazement of the Citizens, who vowed they would never come out again.[12]

The defeat forced the Royalists firmly on to the defensive, and was quickly, though coincidentally, followed by a change in command. Will Legge was recalled to become governor of Oxford, and Byron 'was persuaded by my friends' as he wrote later with rather unconvincing reluctance, to –

> take a commission from His Highness Prince Rupert for the government of Chester, which (though otherwise unwilling) I thought fit to do to avoid such disputes for the future as had formerly happened during Colonel Legg's command there, both to his Majestie's disservice, and my own great trouble and vexation.[13]

In December 1644 Sir John Owen of Clennau, an experienced soldier who had served in the Oxford Army, was appointed high sheriff of Caernarvonshire and governor of the town and castle of Conway. In effect, though subject to Byron's overall command, Owen now military commander in North Wales.

Owen's arrival was unwelcome to Archbishop John Williams, who resented what he saw as a threat to his position in North Wales, but Byron welcomed the arrival of a fellow soldier, who he hoped would bring him more assistance from North Wales than had hitherto been the case. Friction between Byron and the civilian authorities there had been increased by the dislike for Wales and all things Welsh which Byron seems to have conceived from the moment of his arrival in the area, worsened by his tactlessness and lack of understanding for local feeling. On 29 January Byron wrote to Owen, complaining about the weakness of the Chester garrison, and saying that he had made 'journies and written volumes of letters to Wales, and only received promises but no performance to help Chester.'[14]

Brereton meanwhile, on 26 January, had made another probing attack on the outworks of Chester, which was easily driven off by an alert garrison. However in an ultimately more threatening move, three days later Sir William sent a strong force of horse and foot to seize Holt Bridge and occupy Wrexham, once again threatening to isolate Chester.

Byron urgently sought assistance from Owen to counter this move. He had already sent for help to Rupert's younger brother, Prince Maurice, now commanding on the Welsh Border. He hoped that in the meanwhile Owen would convince the Royalist authorities in North Wales of the need to take action 'and advise them rather to march to the frontiers of their country and repell the rebels there rather than to admit them to their bowels.'[15]

Sir John responded as best he could, ordering the Caernarvonshire Trained Bands to rendezvous at Conway 'to attend the motions of the rebels.' But even when reinforced by the Denbighshire and Flintshire Trained Bands, and the three regiments of horse under Byron's command, they were neither willing nor well enough trained and equipped to present a serious threat to Brereton.[16]

In Chester itself, further defence measures were being taken, with £100 of the city plate earmarked to be converted into coin (a mint was maintained at Chester from early in the war). A further weekly assessment was agreed 'for

35. Sir John Owen (1600–66). Owen raised a regiment in North Wales for the King's army in 1642, and served for the next year with the Oxford Army before returning to North Wales. A dedicated Royalist, Owen was regarded by Byron as the most reliable of the Welsh leadership.

36. Prince Maurice (1620–52). Younger brother of Prince Rupert, Maurice is usually overshadowed by him. He was, however, a competent soldier, though lacking his brother's charisma.

perfecting the works, providing match, coals and candles and other necessaries for the use of the garrison.'[17]

Brereton, whilst not particularly alarmed by the activities of the local Welsh Royalists, was concerned at the imminent prospect of intervention by more experienced troops under Prince Maurice. The latter, drawing in men from Royalist garrisons in Staffordshire and Shropshire, and especially from Shrewsbury, had mustered a force of about 2,000 men, with whom he arrived at Ruthin on 17 February. Fearing an attack on their rear by Byron's troops in Chester, the Parliamentarians retreated back to the English side of the Dee.

Chester was again open on its Welsh side, but Maurice, a competent enough soldier though without his brother's genius for war, lacked the strength and confidence to challenge Brereton's dominance in Cheshire. He limited himself to launching a number of raids across the Dee, making use of a bridge of boats positioned near Holt Castle. Of a type said not previously to have been seen in England, it consisted of a boat moored at either bank, with ropes running between them on which was stretched stiff canvas, strong enough to support three men marching abreast.

Any Royalist satisfaction at Maurice's tenuous relief of Chester proved to be short-lived, resulting as it did in disaster elsewhere. On 22 February Parliamentarian forces taking advantage of the absence of so many of the garrison with Maurice, stormed Shrewsbury. Chester was left more vulnerable than ever, and the whole Royalist position along the Welsh border was in serious peril.

Whilst his men worsened the situation by their ferocious plundering of friend and foe alike, Maurice was in Chester, taking further measures for its defence.

Seeing that the outworks were still too extensive for the limited numbers of troops available to defend them, Maurice reduced them again:

> to a narrower compass from the backside of the Tanner's ditches to Cowlane Gate and along the walls of the citty under the Phoenix Tower to the Northgate ditch; and Morgan's mount was made on the other side of the Northgate over against the Goblin's Tower. And all the buildings belonging to the Hospitall of St John's with the Chapel were razed to the ground for fear of sheltering of the enemy.[18]

The suburbs of Great Boughton and, when it eventually fell back into Royalist hands, Chrisleton, were burnt 'in revenge of treachery'.

Fear of betrayal to the enemy was a constant theme among Civil War commanders, and on 4 March Maurice instructed the Royalist leadership in Chester to impose an oath of loyalty on all those within the city, swearing that they would:

> with the utmost of my power, maintain and defend his Majesty's cause against the said rebels, and those who are in arms without his Majesty's express command and consent…[19]

Brereton had by now been reinforced by troops from Lancashire and Yorkshire, and was confident of his ability to meet Maurice in battle, but complained that:

> the enemy declines fighting, and the prisoners say they will not before the rest of their expected forces are united to them…[20]

On 17 March Maurice linked up with Rupert at Ellesmere in Shropshire, and their united forces, about 7,000 strong, returned to Cheshire.

Brereton, despite his own pleas and strenuous efforts by the Committee of Both Kingdoms, had failed to obtain hoped-for assistance from the Scots army in the north of England, or from local Parliamentarian commanders pre-occupied with regional interests. So, in obedience to orders from Westminster, he abandoned operations against Chester as Rupert approached, and fell back to his strongholds of Middlewich and Nantwich.

The Royalists spread out across the countryside, foraging, and on 17 March relieved Beeston Castle, which was held by the resolute Captain William Vallett, of Byron's regiment of horse, who reported: 'No distress; plenty of meat, only little fire or beer.'[21]

The princes and their troops were urgently needed elsewhere, however, and, with Brereton out of easy reach, Rupert's main concern was to obtain reinforcements for the coming spring campaign. He pressed 1,000 new recruits from war-weary North Wales, and to Byron's chagrin, drew off 1,200 men from Chester's garrison. They included the last of the English foot from Ireland, and Prince Rupert's Bluecoats. The arrival of 100 more native Irish foot under Lieutenant-Colonel Little to reinforce Lord Byron's regiment of foot was poor compensation.

Brereton had frustrations of his own. The Scots still refused to join with him in attacking Rupert's withdrawing forces, so that he complained:

> It doth much afflict and vex me that these armies are retreated and not encountered, though God hath delivered us from their fury and cruelty, yet I fear they will do mischief elsewhere if God restrain them not. Were I guilty or accessory my grief would be much increased… I am persuaded a heavy judgement is reserved for them and whoever encounters them shall prevail, their sin being so ripe. But seeing the Lord doth not judge us worthy of the honour to be the instruments of his vengeance, his will be done.[22]

By early April he had resumed operations on the English side of Chester, sending parties of horse across the Dee from Wirral at low tide, probably in the vicinity of Shotwick, to raid Royalist cavalry quarters and drive herds of looted cattle back from Flintshire.

Byron's own problems were growing. He wrote gloomily on 3 April to Prince Rupert:

> the want of your Highness's presence in these parts, (though occasioned by inevitable accidents) and the continuance of the Rebells' army so neere unto us hath begot so much despaire amongst all people here, that unless some speedy hope of reliefe be given them, I much feare… a general revolt…[23]

Morale in Chester must have sunk still lower next day, when Brereton's horse crossed into Wales again, and, leaving a detachment to blockade Hawarden Castle, approached the suburb of Handbridge. A Royalist outpost at Manley House was reduced, and Handbridge pillaged, and then, yet again, burnt on Byron's orders:

to prevent the enemy from nesting there, as were all the Glovers' houses under the Walls by Dee Side and the houses without the Watergate.[24]

Brereton, despite ongoing difficulties in keeping his men well enough paid and supplied to prevent unauthorised plundering, had tightened his blockade by establishing new outposts along the Dee south of Chester at Eccleston, Lache and Dodleston, and was confident that the city would soon be forced to surrender, being,

> so blocked up and straitened that no manner of provision can be conveyed to them on either side [of the Dee]. They are so sensible of this that they begin to stint the inhabitants to one meal a day, although they have only been debarred from two markets on this side of the river. It is said fire, salt and hay are much wanting, and I am confident that, if our wants be supplied and we are not interrupted, before many weeks their wants will bring them to a better understanding.[25]

But conditions in Chester were probably not quite as bad as Brereton believed, and the Parliamentarian commander found his efforts increasingly frustrated by his own shortages of troops and supplies, for most of the available men had either already been enlisted or had made themselves scarce to avoid conscription.

> and for money they are so far exhausted betwixt free quartering of our own and plundering by the enemy, their daily taxations and their weekly mises for those garrisons that they are subject to, that they profess that, being restrained from selling that little cheese which is most of their sustenance, they are not able to contribute any more unless they should sell the very clothes off their backs and their wives and childrens...[26]

Numbers of Brereton's men, especially the auxiliary troops from neighbouring counties, were deserting or in a state of near-mutiny, looting Welsh cattle and selling them for their own profit, or in the case of his own men, threatening to return to their homes in order to fight their Yorkshire 'allies', who were busily pillaging parts of Parliamentarian-held Cheshire. The defection of so many troops left Brereton sorely stretched to maintain his blockade.

Supplies were still slipping into Chester by boat along the River Dee. They were difficult to prevent, for as Lieutenant-Colonel Coote angrily warned Brereton on 21 April:

you must take some better course to besiege Chester by sea than by a stinking boat or two that are not able to do any good.[27]

But Sir William might have been encouraged if he had seen a lengthy letter written by Byron on 26 April to Lord George Digby:

I know that is usual for men to exaggerate the importance of those places where their commands lie, but without any such self-partiality this place stands unrivalled in relation to his Majesty's affairs. The two princes having united their forces and relieved Beeston Castle were earnestly entreated by me to clear this country before they departed of the petty garrisons which infested Chester, but other considerations at that time hindered the effecting of it and therefore with a promise that the army should continue within a distance, till Chester were furnished both with victuals and ammunition, I was contented to return and undertake the government of that garrison. But the business of Hereford interfering, Prince Rupert was suddenly called away before either ammunition or victual could be brought into Chester, and together with his Highness marched away the remainder of the old Irish regiments with some other horse and foot to the number of at least 1,200, so that I was left in the town with only a garrison of citizens and my own and Colonel Mostin's regiments, which both together made not above 600 men, whereof one half being Mostin's men, I was forced soon after to

37. George, Lord Digby (1612–77). Generally regarded as an ambitious intriguer, Digby became a secretary of state in 1643, and was eventually a leading opponent of Prince Rupert, using against him considerable influence with the King.

send out of town, finding them by reason of their officers, who were ignorant Welsh gentlemen and unwilling to undergo any strict duty, far more prejudicial to us than useful. The rebels, finding the Prince retreated with his army and the country emptied of all soldiers but such as were necessary for keeping the garrisons, returned with all their forces to block up Chester on all sides which ever since they have continued, and withal laid siege to Hawarden Castle. The Welsh though they have men for number and army sufficient to beat the rebels out of Wales, yet either will not or dare not stir, notwithstanding the many orders I have sent them. The truth is that so long as that cursed Commission of Array or at least such Commissioners as are put into it have any power there, the King must expect no good out of North Wales, and I am confident were it not for the castles which are well provided both with men victual and ammunition that country would long since have taken part with Brereton and Middleton. Thus you see I am left in a condition neither to offend others nor defend myself, if pressed by a considerable army… Besides this, if speedy relief come not, the want of gunpowder will be sufficient to blow me up there, there not being full 18 barrels in store neither any public magazine of victual nor money for public service. I have the more fully related my condition to your Lordship to the end that if any misfortune should befall me before relief come, it may appear how little accessory I have been to it; and for these poor means I have left to maintain this place, you may be assured I shall improve them to the utmost, and how unfortunate soever I may be, you shall have an account of my charge befitting an honest man and one whom I hope you shall not blush to own.[28]

There is little doubt that Byron's letter, which reached Digby as the Royalist Council of War was making final plans for the summer campaign, played an important part in the decision to make the relief of Chester and the recovery of the north of England, rather than encountering the Parliamentarian New Model Army, the main objective of the Oxford Army.

By early May Brereton was confident that Chester would soon fall unless relief came, and he also continued to press his blockade of Beeston and more active siege operations at Hawarden Castle, where mining operations were under way. The governor of Hawarden, Sir William Neale, was away, but his wife, Lady Helen, was determined to hold out to the last, as she informed her husband in a letter of 9 May:

38. Lady Neale. Many women of all classes found themselves caught up in the war when their homes were besieged. They often played an important inspirational role in their defence.

My Hart, I wonder infinitely that sending for intelligence I could not heare from you. Our condition is at this tyme very desperate for besides the approach of their myne which is very neare ye great Round Tower they have brought over great peeces for five carriages we discovered, but whether they be all for Battery wee know not because ye worke they are making for one of them is conceived by ye Captaine for a mortar piece… I am purposed to hould out as longe as there is meate for man for none of these eminent dangers shall ever frighten mee from my loyalty but in life and death I will be ye King's faithfull subject and thy constant lovinge wife and humble servant,

Helen Neale.[29]

But fortune was rapidly turning against Brereton. On 16 May James Lothian reported that the defenders of Hawarden had detected the mine shaft by countermining, and had broken into the tunnel and blocked it. Michael Jones scarcely concealed his dissatisfaction with the way Brereton was conducting operations, sending him a stream of advice on troop deployments and informing Sir William, who under the terms of the self-denying ordnance would as an MP shortly have to return to Westminster: 'If you manage this business well and give ye King and Princes a defeat you will be continued your command.'[30]

The decision as to whether to persist with operations at Hawarden was left to the commanders on the spot, and at a council of war on 17 May, hearing that the Oxford Army had advanced to Newport in Shropshire, they voted by a majority of seven to one to abandon operations on the Welsh side of the Dee and withdraw to Nantwich.[31] The retreat, partly over a bridge of boats near Eccleston, and partly over the Dee fords near Shotwick, where the foot crossed up to their middles in water, was carried out successfully, with little interference from the Royalists, crippled by their shortage of powder. Only Colonel Marcus Trevor and his cavalry carried out some harassing operations, taking several naked Parliamentarian troopers prisoners as they were bathing in Pulford Brook.[32]

But, although Brereton expressed satisfaction on extricating his men from a potentially dangerous situation with little loss, the fact remained that his first major attempt to reduce Chester had ended in failure, and all must be done over again.

5

CHESTER SURPRISED: JUNE–SEPTEMBER 1645

With the threat from Brereton for the moment greatly reduced, Byron hoped that the King would take advantage of the opportunity to reduce the remaining Parliamentarian strongholds in Cheshire and repeat Rupert's invasion of Lancashire of the previous year, confidently promising him 5,000 recruits there.[1] However, despite putting forward his reasons in person to the Royalist council of war at Stone in Staffordshire, Byron was unable to dissuade them from moving on eastwards, initially with the aim of reducing pressure on the Royalist capital of Oxford by attacking Leicester. Byron's pleas that the troops taken from him in the spring should be returned were also unsuccessful; indeed he had to reinforce the field army with Robert Werden's horse.

> I then humbly besought his Majesty to discharge me of his command and [let me serve] as a volunteer in his army, rather than condemn me to so comfortless an Employment where I had neither men, money nor ammunition to defend the places committed to my charge. But neither in that particular would his Majesty grant my request, but commanded me to return to Chester, with assurance of speedy and plentiful supplies out of Ireland, and withal, that so long as his Army was on foot, it was probable that the Rebels would not attempt anything upon me, but rather draw all their forces after him.[2]

Though 'infinitely against my own sense', a gloomy Byron returned to Chester, and began to take what steps he could to strengthen the defences. He made plans for a fort at Handbridge, designed to prevent besiegers from closing in around the southern end of the Dee Bridge, as they had done in previous attacks. It would prove to be a formidable addition to Chester's fortifications. Although its exact site and dimensions are unknown, it was probably a 'sconce', a square fort with an angle bastion at each corner.[3] But few funds were available either for the fort 'or anything else that was requisite for the defence of Chester', so Byron went to Denbigh:

> whither I summoned all the Commissioners of Array and Gentry of the five counties of North Wales, and having propounded such things to them as requisite both for his Majesty's service and their own preservation, found (according to the custom of that land of promise but never of performance) a ready assent to almost anything I could desire of them… This being done, I returned to Chester, where not long after I received the sad news of the fatal blow given at Naseby.[4]

There, on 14 June, the King's summer campaign had ended in a crushing defeat at the hands of the New Model Army. Byron knew that the effective

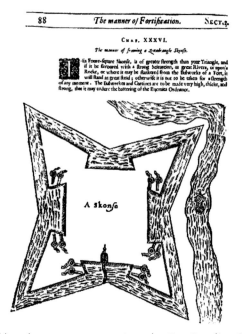

39. A 'sconce'. Although no trace now survives, the 'Fort Royal' at Chester was almost certainly of the type of fortification known as a 'sconce'. Constructed from earth, with a ditch and topped by wooden palisades, a sconce might contain several guns, and, if properly constructed and garrisoned, could be quite formidable.

destruction of the principal Royalist field army meant that Chester would ultimately be in greater danger than ever before.

In the short term, however, the city was not directly threatened. Brereton, as an MP, had been disqualified by Parliament's self-denying ordnance from holding military command, and he had now returned to Westminster. Direction of affairs in Cheshire had devolved upon the county committee, led by Sir George Booth, Philip Mainwaring and Lord Stanley of Alderley. The committee members were mostly Presbyterian, without Brereton's strong religious motivation – indeed his puritanism had been one of the reasons they sought to replace him. They lacked his enthusiasm and energy, and, although purely military affairs were left in the hands of the professionals, Michael Jones and James Lothian, there was a noticeable slackening in the pace of operations for most of the summer.

Troops were drawn away for service elsewhere, and various alarms resulting from the King's erratic peregrinations after Naseby prevented Jones and Lothian from undertaking any serious attack on Chester, although outposts were maintained at Hooton and Tarvin, and Beeston remained loosely blockaded. In a sign of renewed activity, the leaguer of Beeston was stepped up at the end of July, when the Parliamentarians constructed a fort within musket shot of the castle gate, which enabled them to keep up a tight blockade using only a small force.[5]

Byron was meanwhile spending a frustrating summer. Promised contributions from North Wales were slow in materialising, and he was further distracted by a prolonged dispute over the quartering of other Royalist forces in the area supposedly under his own command. After another threat of resignation, and personal visits to the King and Prince Rupert, matters were eventually settled to Byron's satisfaction, but his attention had been distracted from Chester. On returning, Byron found 'nothing done neither at the fort designed at Handbridge nor at the powder mills which were formerly gone to ruin.'[6] He was next forced to make another journey into North Wales where Sir John Owen and Archbishop Williams were openly at odds, and Merionethshire threatened with incursions by Sir Thomas Myddleton's Parliamentarian forces from Montgomeryshire.

For some of what follows we are dependent on Byron's own version of events, which should of course be treated with some caution. Lord John claimed that before leaving for North Wales, he had drawn the attention of the mayor, Charles Walley, and the deputy governor, Sir Francis Gamull, to the laxness and inadequate numbers of the guard maintained on the outworks. He had toured the defences with Walley, and pointed out to him:

those works where I conceived the most danger to be of a surprisal, and particularly a place near the river (where afterwards the enemy entered) and gave order that it should be palisadoed, and that the ditch should be made wider and deeper, and that a guard house should be built there for the better security of the place. I likewise gave order for the pulling down of St John's steeple, which (in case the Rebels should possess the suburbs) would be very prejudicial to the city as overlooking it, and from whence (in the ensuing siege) was received our greatest annoyance. All these things the Mayor promised to see done, but performed none of them.[7]

Whatever the truth of the matter, these defects must have been obvious for some time, and Byron must share the responsibility for the failure to deal with them earlier.

Whilst staying at Mostyn Hall in Flintshire completing discussions with the county commissioners of array, Byron received a report, which had also been sent to Sir Francis Gamull, that the enemy had gathered larger than usual forces at Tarvin, and that 'it was much suspected that they had some design upon Chester.' Byron warned the garrison to be on the alert, but did not immediately return himself. He claimed that, either through treachery or apathy, no additional precautions were taken, and in any case by the time Byron's warning arrived on 19 September it may well have been too late.[8]

The apparent lack of action for much of the summer by the Parliamentarian forces in Cheshire was providing ammunition for Brereton's supporters in the county. Moves were afoot to restore him to command, and it may have been reports of this which stung the Cheshire leaders into action.

On 19 September, amidst great secrecy, they drew off from the forces before Beeston a contingent of 500 horse, 200 dragoons and 700 foot. Using narrow byways and quiet lanes so that no word of their approach should reach Chester, the Parliamentarians made 'a tedious march' through the night, and appeared before the outworks of Chester at dawn the next day. Such probes were not unusual, and the Royalist sentry who sighted them was not apparently unduly perturbed, shouting sarcastically to ask 'if we had brought our dear bretheren (meaning the Scots) with us, to take the Citie'.[9]

However this initial approach was merely a diversion, under cover of which a party of soldiers with scaling ladders slipped along the river bank up to the fort nearest to the Dee, known as the Gun Mount, and stormed it. The defenders, mainly men of Gamull's regiment, were caught almost completely unprepared. The Parliamentarian assault was spearheaded by Brereton's firelocks, ironically in some cases the same men who had served with Captain

40. Storming the 'mount'. Though Byron suggested that treachery had played a part in the loss of the suburbs, it seems more likely that the defenders panicked when taken by surprise. Note the wooden 'storm poles' intended to hinder this kind of attack.

Thomas Sandford in Ireland and at the capture of Beeston in the previous year. They had been captured at Nantwich, and had changed sides en masse. Their commander, Captain Gimbert,

> was the first that entered, his ladder being too short, he lift up his man to the mount, (neere the riverside) from the top of it, his man drew him up by the hand, and then they cryde a towne a towne, immediately they cleared that Mount, slew Lieutenant Aldersley, the Captaine of the Watch, and put the rest, about six men, to flight, then others set too their ladders, possest themselves of all the Mounts on that side the Citie, and with the instruments wee brought with us, brake open the gates: then all the Horse entered, with the remainder of the Foot, with loude shouts, which utterly daunted the enemy.[10]

Despite later accusations by Byron of treachery, and the brief arrest of Captain William Barnston of Gamull's regiment, in reality the Parliamentarian assault, which began between 2 and 3 a.m., had completely surprised the defenders. Parliamentarian troops poured into the streets and lanes of the suburbs, such little resistance as was mounted crumbling before them, as the panic-stricken citizens fled towards the inner defences formed by the old city walls, taking with them such few possessions as they could collect together quickly. Walley abandoned his sword, mace of office and wife in his haste. A brief attempt at a stand was made near the Bars, but was outflanked by attackers pressing on through the houses on either side. The Royalists only just managed to close the great Eastgate in the face of the enemy, who had captured at a stroke all of the eastern and possibly most of the northern suburbs of Chester, and who now began preparations to press home their attack on the inner defences.[11]

The Parliamentarians had to some extent been surprised by the degree of their success, and the Cheshire committee now sent urgently for assistance to neighbouring counties. Their pleas were backed by the Committee of Both Kingdoms, which wrote on 26 September to the county committee in Stafford:

> you must have heard of the taking of the suburbs of Chester and know the importance to our N.W. parts to have that place reduced. We therefore desire you to send all the force you can spare with your own safety, to assist in that undertaking before the place receive further reinforcements from the enemy, which may render it more difficult of accomplishment. We are informed of the march of the King's forces that way and have given order to follow them closely, which we doubt not will prevent the besiegers from being interrupted by the enemy's forces…[12]

Letters in similar vein were sent other local commanders, whilst General Sydenham Poyntz, commanding the troops from the Parliamentarian Northern Association who had been tasked with shadowing the King and his remaining cavalry wherever they went, was given specific instructions:

> We have information that the King, with most of his forces is marched towards Chester. If he be not closely followed our forces that have lately so happily surprised the suburbs and are in a fair way to take the town will be endangered. Chester is a place of very real consequence both for the reducing and settling of all North Wales and for preventing the landing of any Irish supplies. We desire to thank you for your diligence in following the King's party hitherto and now would have you to follow them so closely that they may not be able to give any impediment to the progress of the works before Chester.[13]

Both sides were engaged in a race against time, the Parliamentarians hoping to complete the capture of Chester before the King's forces could intervene, and the defenders to hold out until help arrived.

The garrison hastily blocked up the Eastgate with earth and dung, and sent urgent word of their plight to Byron, still at Mostyn Hall. The Royalist commander ordered his host, Roger Mostyn, to bring his regiment of foot, dismissed from the Chester garrison in April, back into the city, and also sent for Colonel Hugh Wynne's regiment, currently in Merionethshire. Returning in haste to Chester, Byron found:

> all things in such confusion, that had the Rebels attempted it, they might have carried the City as well as the Suburbs. For though all the City were in arms yet knew they not how to dispose of them or in what place to use them to best advantage, but ranged up and down the street in promiscuous bodies, and would fain have done something, but knew not how to go about it.[14]

The Royalists had attempted a sally, but confusion and a delay of several hours occurred when the key to open the gate of the sally port could not be found. When a contingent of Gamull's men finally advanced, 'the service is very hot and the enemy in much more readiness than was expected'. After losing three dead and three wounded, the Royalists hastily withdrew, whilst:

> Captain Adlington, who, standing on the wall to behold the skirmish, was shot through the crown of his hat without doing him any harm at all.[15]

Byron took immediate steps to get to grips with the crisis:

> To remedy all these disorders, immediately upon my arrival I called all the officers together, and appointed them their several posts, and what guards should be kept; and withal, what Officers, Gentlemen and Reformadoes (of which there was then a good store in Town) should upon all occasions be assistant at such and such places. I likewise gave order to the Mayor presently to provide all such materials as were requisite for a Town besieged as Spades, Mattocks, Shovels, Links, lanthorns, pitched ropes, with divers other necessaries, (whereof I gave him a list in writing) and that he should have them in readiness at the pent-house, a place where we kept our main guard. I called also all the Artificers, firemen and granado men together, and gave to each their several charges, and where they should keep their stations. The people generally expressed great joy upon my coming into Town, and seemed much heartened therewith, and voluntarily entered (from the highest to the lowest) into a mutual obligation, both of supporting me in the charge of the siege, and suffering with me to the last, in both which undertakings they afterwards failed. I thought to have taken advantage of this their

alacrity (knowing well how soon the heat of such motions useth to cool) and by a resolute Sally to have attempted the beating of the Enemy out of the Suburbs: but they having drawn in more forces both of horse and foot (in regard of the vicinity of their garrisons) and strongly barricaded the streets, and the horse and foot which I had sent for (which were more remote) not being yet come, I was dissuaded from it, and advised not to put things to so great hazard. So that all that could be done for the present, was with fire arrows to burn a number of thatched houses that stood near unto the wall, and for the more substantial houses (which annoyed us extremely and overtopped the walls) I hired three desperate fellows to burn them. But the Citizens (most of whom had tenements in the Suburbs) could not endure to see their houses on fire, and therefore gave what impediment they could to such endeavours.[16]

Most of the property burnt was around Cow Lane, St John's Lane and St Thomas Street near the Northgate, which reduced the cover available to the besiegers, 'And thereby room given to our marksmen from the walls and towers to show their skill, which they did with that dexterity as almost hourly one or other of them dropt.'[17]

By now nightfall was approaching, and amidst the flames of the burning houses in the suburbs 'the whole city big with expectation of a sudden storm, stand armed for a brave resistance.'[18]

In what would prove a particular annoyance to the defenders, the Parliamentarians stationed snipers and a small gun in the steeple of St John's Church, not far from the Newgate 'which did us some little annoyance, and hindered our walking in some streets or places of the city which it did command.'[19]

After a relative lull on Sunday 21 September, fighting resumed in earnest at about noon the next day. The Parliamentarians had brought up two or more guns, probably demi-culverins, from Tarvin and Nantwich, and, under cover of some undemolished houses, established them in a battery near St John's Church, within a 'pistol shot' (about 200 yards), of a 'Decayed piece of the wall' near Newgate.[20]

Byron, as he admitted, was taken by surprise:

So that until their first gun played (which was about noon) I had no intelligence of their intention. Upon the hearing of which, I immediately came to the place, by which time they had made two or three holes through the upper part of the wall. I found a great concourse of people there, but so terrified with the great guns, and the small shot which from St Johns Steeple they hurt and killed many of them, that at first I found much ado to make them to stand, till after a while, recollecting themselves, they fell to work, seeing the wall fall so fast that it was high time to do it. Major [Humphrey] Sydenham and one [George] Loope (formerly an officer of the Trayne, and then Comptroller of the Ordnance at Chester) were chief instruments in the ordering and making up of the breach, and the three desperate soldiers before mentioned, were main actors in it, two whereof were slain there and the third sorely wounded, but afterwards recovered. I must not forget the diligence of one [Randle] Holmes, an Alderman of the City, who brought woolpacks and feather beds from all parts of the town to stop up the breach which with great industry and pains was made defensible against their battery so that towards the town it was very high and precipitous; but on the battering side towards the Enemy was made so flat by reason of the crumbling of the soft stone, and so wide, that six horses might have marched up in rank, which I believe was the reason that invited them afterwards to storm it so boldly.[21]

Throughout the bombardment Byron kept the walls manned and reserves on alert in various parts of the town, in case the Parliamentarians used the distraction of the cannonade to make an assault in another place.

41. Transporting guns. Although light and medium guns could be moved fairly easily by road in good weather, transporting heavy artillery was a major undertaking. Heavy siege guns were most easily moved by water.

42. Battery position. The Parliamentarian gun battery which created the breach in the wall near Newgate was probably sited in the area of trees beyond the Roman amphitheatre.

At about 4 p.m., after firing thirty-two shots (suggesting that two guns were probably in use) the bombardment ceased. A breach had been made in the wall about 200 yards south of the Newgate, which modern measurements suggest to have been about 25ft wide, confirming Byron's estimate.[22]

The defenders expected an immediate assault, but for some unexplained reason, possibly difficulty organising an assault force, a lull of four hours followed, so that Byron began to believe that no attack would be made. But:

> [At] about eight a clocke at night and faire moonshine, we perceive two bodies of an army advance towards us, the one of which attempts to skale upon the east between the Sadler's tower and the Eastgate, where they were flanked by the said towers...[23]

The attack was spearheaded by the firelock companies of Captain Sion Finch (probably an ex-Royalist officer from Ireland captured at Nantwich) and Captain Gimbert, and many of those taking part were also part of the English contingent from Ireland. Byron admitted that the attackers came on with 'great boldness', but he had taken precautions to meet the assault. Positioned around the breach were Captain Thropp and Lieutenant King's companies of Gamull's regiment, while:

> those in the Newgate and the houses adjoining to the breach, annoyed the Enemy with their shot, so did the granadoes and the fire pikes,

which were used by very stout men, and placed upon the flanks of the breach. Captain Crosby (who commanded the Chirk horse) did good service there, and the Rebels pressed on so resolutely that I caused more forces to be drawn down to assist Major Thropp's men. Thrice that night the Enemy was upon the top of the wall, but at last quite beaten off; seven of them were killed upon the top of the wall, who afterwards fell into the Street, and were the next day buried by us. There were some of them taken alive, but much hurt, and so drunk, that the scent of them was very offensive. On our part were slain six common soldiers, and three officers of horse shot (who afterwards died of their wounds) which were Captain Crosby's Lieutenant, Cornet and Corporal. The Enemy for certain lost upon that service their Regiment of firelocks (who first entered the suburbs) to a very small number, besides divers others. At the same time they attempted to scale the walls at a place called Saddler's Tower, but were immediately beaten off by Col. Mostyn's men.[24]

The attackers had apparently been fortified prior to the assault by being given a mixture of aqua vita (brandy) and gunpowder to drink. Randle Holme credits the Chirk horse, fighting on foot with sword and pistol, with the main role in beating off the assault. The enemy had gained a foothold in the breach:

43. View from Parliamentarian battery. Looking from the approximate position of the Parliamentarian guns, the old Newgate (now the 'Wolf Gate') is to the right of the modern Newgate. The breach is obscured by the modern wall (left centre).

44. Firelock. Armed with flintlock muskets, more reliable, though more expensive, than the matchlock, 'firelock' troops were often regarded as élite forces, used for various special missions. Many of those serving with the Parliamentarians at Chester were ex-Royalist troops from the English army in Ireland.

our men beat back, but by the courage of the Chirk Castle troope, which lighting from their saddles with sword and pistol regained what the enemy had won, who reattempt the passage, but were reinforct to a retreat and at last to disorder... indeed Captain Crosby with his troupe deserves remembrance, who having charge of the horse guard, behaved himself so bravely that some of our bouldest enemies took their death upon, he was a souldier...[25]

The Parliamentarian assault had narrowly failed, partly because of the reluctance to advance of many of the troops intended to support the firelocks, and the fact that some of the scaling ladders were too short. But as the Parliamentarians themselves admitted, Royalist resistance was so fierce that the attack had in any case little chance of success. Casualties, though probably not as heavy as Royalist accounts suggest, are unknown.[26]

The defenders of Chester had gained a breathing space, but their situation remained critical, and it was with great relief that they greeted Byron's uncle, Sir Nicholas, when he came into the city on the Welsh side that same evening with news that the King and a relief force was approaching. On the events of the next few hours might hang the fate of Royalist Chester.

6

THE BATTLE OF ROWTON HEATH: 24 SEPTEMBER 1645

In retrospect the battle of Naseby represents more clearly the death of Royalist hopes than was apparent at the time. The King still had substantial forces in the field in the west of England, whilst his champion in Scotland, the Marquis of Montrose, was winning a string of victories. Charles had also salvaged some 4,000 cavalry from the debacle at Naseby, and these retained considerable nuisance value, as well as a potential cadre around which to build a new field army.

The defeat of the Royalist western forces at Langport (10 July) was a serious blow to their hopes of a recovery in England, and the attention of Charles and his more sanguine advisers switched to Scotland, where Montrose appeared on the brink of decisive victory. A first attempt to march north to join him got no further than Doncaster in Yorkshire, where the King was forced to turn back when threatened with being trapped between the Scots horse under David Leslie and the forces of the Parliamentarian Northern Association under Colonel-General Sydenham Poyntz.

Temporarily frustrated, the King and his cavalry eventually made their way back to Raglan Castle in South Wales, whilst Poyntz was ordered to shadow their movements. Urged on by his over-optimistic secretary of state, Lord George Digby, and in any case lacking any practicable military alternative, King Charles once more turned his thoughts towards linking up with Montrose. On 18 September, with no clear plan beyond somehow linking up with the Royalist forces in Scotland, the King and his horse, about 3,500 strong, set off northwards along the Welsh Border.

45. Sydenham Poyntz (d.*c*.1660). A London apprentice who became a professional soldier in Europe during the Thirty Years' War, Poyntz was a ruthless officer who returned to England in 1645 to command Parliament's Army of the Northern Association, possibly more with a view to financial reward than from political conviction.

Poyntz, currently in the Leominster area of Herefordshire, was temporarily evaded, and the Royalists pushed on across the hills of Radnorshire and Montgomery, reaching Chirk Castle on 21 September. Here the King's plans were dramatically altered by the news of the loss of the Chester suburbs.

Considering their next move, the King and his commanders were no doubt updated on the current situation by messages from Byron and by patrols sent out by Sir Richard Lloyd from Holt Castle. The plan they settled on was designed to bolster the resistance of the Chester garrison whilst at the same time trapping the besiegers, believed to number about 500 horse and 1,500 foot, in the captured suburbs before they could retreat behind the defences of Tarvin.[1]

The King divided his force. Charles himself, with his own and Lord Gerrard's lifeguards, and Colonel Herbert Price's regiment of Gerrard's brigade, perhaps 600 men in all, marched directly to Chester along the Welsh bank of the Dee and crossed into the city via the Dee Bridge, arriving, 'tired and overmarcht', on the evening of 23 September. Charles lodged for the night in the Lower Bridge Street house of Sir Francis Gamull, where he doubtless conferred with Byron and his officers.[2]

Meanwhile the remainder of the Royalist army, consisting of perhaps 3,000 horse under their major-general, Sir Marmaduke Langdale, crossed the Dee at Holt, using either Holt Bridge itself or a bridge of boats further upstream.

46. Sir Marmaduke Langdale (1598?–1661). A leading Yorkshire Royalist, who was a brigade commander in the Northern Royalist army until Marston Moor, after which he took command of the Northern Horse. A dour and formidable character, allegedly 'much in love with his own judgement', Langdale earned the devotion of his unruly troopers.

Marching across country via Churton and Aldford, Langdale reached the Chester–Whitchurch road about a mile south of the village of Saighton, and bivouacked for the night on Hatton Heath, 5 miles south-east of Chester.

Langdale intended to resume his march early next morning (24 September) once daylight provided him with better knowledge of enemy movements. His aim remained either to trap the besiegers in the suburbs of Chester, or hit them in the flank as they attempted to withdraw to Tarvin. Lord Digby, with the King in Chester, claimed that a Parliamentarian withdrawal had already begun:

> The rebels… on intelligence of our approach, drew off their cannon and were preparing to march away, when on the sudden they drew their cannon back again, and showed they were resolved to maintain the post which they had gotten, which we conjectured either to be despair of their retreat, or that they had intelligence of approaching relief.[3]

The second supposition was the correct one. Whilst making their plans the Royalists had apparently ignored the possibility of intervention by Poyntz. They appear to have assumed that they had given him the slip during the course of their march, but in fact the Parliamentarian commander was still sticking closely to their heels.

47. Charles, Lord Gerrard (d.1690). A Lancashire Royalist who fought in the Oxford
Army before being appointed to command in South Wales in 1644. His harsh methods
alienated the local population, and Gerard was removed in August 1645 and made
lieutenant-general of horse.

On the same night that King Charles entered Chester, Poyntz, with about
3,000 horse drawn from the Northern Association and the Midlands, 'tired
with long marches from before' was entering Whitchurch, 15 miles to the
south. Here he encountered messengers sent in search of him by the Cheshire
commanders, and replied with a promise of immediate assistance. It was this
message which caused the Cheshire forces to reverse their retreat and to resolve
to hold their position for as long as possible 'upon assurance of Major-General
Poyntz his advance with a considerable body of horse.'[4]

For their part the Royalists seem first to have become aware of Poyntz's
approach when one of his messengers to the Cheshire commanders was
captured by Sir Richard Lloyd's patrols from Holt. The news was sent quickly
to both Langdale and King Charles, and the latter called a hasty council of war
in the early hours of 24 September.

> The result whereof was that His Majesty's Guards, and the Lord
> Gerrard's Horse, with five hundred foot, should be drawn out early the
> next morning at the Northgate suburbs (which were then free) and from
> thence either to join with Sir Marmaduke, or divert such additional
> forces as the Enemy might draw from Chester to join with Poyntz.[5]

It must have been approaching 4 a.m. by the time that this decision was reached, and it may have been up to an hour later before Langdale was informed. He may also have been instructed to withdraw nearer to Chester, so that he could be supported more easily, but it was by now dawn, and Langdale's scouts reported Poyntz's column approaching from the south.

The terrain over which the opening phases of the battle were to be fought consisted mainly of large areas of unenclosed sandy heathland. There were however some small enclosures in the cultivated areas around such small villages as Rowton and Waverton. The area was traversed by a number of lanes, and by the Whitchurch–Chester road, itself no more than a sandy track, lined by hedges in places, such as the point where it crossed from Hatton onto Miller's Heath.

It was probably on Miller's Heath that Langdale drew up his main force. Details of his deployment are lacking, though the Royalists were probably formed into about six divisions, whilst Langdale lined with dragoons the hedges on the road connecting the two areas of heathland.

On this occasion Parliamentarian reconnaissance also seems to have been faulty, for Poyntz apparently did not learn of Langdale's proximity until his vanguard came under fire from the hedgerows. A Parliamentarian account admitted that the two sides met 'before they knew [of] one another.'[6]

Poyntz's troopers were strung out in column of march, and possibly because of the enclosed nature of the terrain at this point, seem to have had difficulty in deploying. Poyntz also seems to have discounted the strength of the opposition, and hoped to force his way through the ambush with a rush using the troops immediately available.

The Parliamentarians 'immediately drew into order, and advanced upon them (though all his force were not then come up).'[7] The vanguard, apparently consisting of Hugh Bethell's and Richard Greave's regiments, together with Poyntz's lifeguard, may by now have too entangled with the Royalist ambuscade to withdraw easily. The main initial encounter took place on the road itself, where the Royalists,

in order confronted our van led by Colonel Hugh Bethell in the midst of a lane betwixt two moors covered with armed men of both Battailes, where was given a very sharp and gallant charge by both parties, for after Pistolls were discharged at half Pikes distance [about 6–8ft] they disputed the matter with their swords a full quarter of an houre, neither yielding ground to the other, until at length the enemy were forced to retreat.[8]

48. Cavalry on the march. It was usual practice in hostile territory to send out patrols ahead of and on the flanks of a column of horse on the march, though it appears that Poyntz neglected to do this in his approach to Chester.

Poyntz followed up along the lane with his 'forlorn hope', probably consisting of his lifeguard; 'he was very active in his own person, very many gallant Gentlemen with him'.[9]

As the Parliamentarians debouched from the mouth of the lane onto the open ground and attempted to deploy, they found themselves under attack from increasing numbers of Royalist horse. Fighting was fierce, as Poyntz's men were:

> re-incountred by a fresh reserve at the Lane's mouth, and they were likewise discomfited, and a third, but being over-powered were in the end forced to retreat in the Lane, incapable of receiving a reserve to second them; here we had some losses, the enemy pursuing to the Lane's end, but were beaten back, for there was space for our reserves to advance [presumably when the advancing Royalists themselves began to come out onto Hatton Heath]. Colonell Bethell and Colonell Greaves were then sore wounded, after this the General perceiving the enemy lay upon his advantage (in a good posture upon the open field) only skirmished him with some flying parties, whilst he held correspondency with his friends in Chester suburbs.[10]

The Parliamentarians had had much the worst of the first encounter, admitting to losing twenty dead, a number of wounded and fifty or sixty prisoners, including Colonel Greaves, together with two or three cavalry colours. Royalist losses were probably somewhat lighter, but if Langdale were to follow up his success reinforcements from Chester were vital, if only to prevent any assistance from the Cheshire forces from reaching Poyntz.

So, possibly at about 8 a.m., Langdale despatched Lieutenant-Colonel Jeffrey Shakerley of Robert Werden's regiment to report to the King. Shakerley was a Cheshire man, who made use of local knowledge to shorten his journey. Riding down to the Dee, he got:

> a wooden tub [used for the slaughtering of swine] and a batting staff [used for batting coarse linen] for a bar, put a servant in the tub with him, and in this desperate manner swam over the river, his horse swimming by him for the banks there were very steep and the river very deep, ordered his servant to stay there with the tub for his return and was with the King in little more than quarter of an hour after he left Sir Marmaduke.[11]

As a result the King and his commanders in Chester must have been aware of Langdale's situation very soon after the first phase of the fighting on Hatton Heath had ended. Unfortunately the contents of Sir Marmaduke's despatch are

49. Crossing the Dee. Shakerley's expedient seems to have been largely wasted because of the delays by the Royalist leadership in Chester. He would be an active royalist conspirator throughout the interregnum.

unknown. He may have been confident of being able to hold off Poyntz, but he must have been concerned about the possibility of the Cheshire Parliamentarians attacking his rear. The garrison of Chester were still expecting to make a sortie, for they were clearing the barriers from behind the Eastgate. This suggests some confusion of intent, for a sortie from this direction would have been designed either to reoccupy the suburbs or harass the rear of the withdrawing besiegers. The Royalists may have been confident that on receiving news of Poyntz's discomfiture, the Cheshire Army would indeed fall back on Tarvin, leaving the way clear for reinforcements to join Langdale. They may in fact have spent some time waiting for this to happen, for the troops in Chester, now under the overall command of the King's lieutenant-general, Lord Charles Gerrard, were too few to recapture the suburbs from a determined opponent.

There were, then, some reasons for the King not to act hastily, but none of them explain the time lapse which actually occurred. Shakerley's account says:

> such delays were made some about the King that no orders were sent, nor any sally made out of the city by the King's party till past three o'clock in the afternoone, which was full six hours after Poyntz had been beaten back.[12]

One problem may have been fatigue among many of the Royalist troops; the King's horse had had little rest for some days, while the garrison had been standing to arms since the surprise of the suburbs. Faced with the prospect of a tougher fight than he had anticipated, Gerrard was critically short of foot, and it is possible that he was waiting for Colonel Hugh Wynne's regiment from North Wales, which arrived in Chester at some point during the day. Byron was also bringing in any other troops he could muster.

Another key factor may well have been the rivalries and jealousies which existed among the Royalist commanders. Gerrard and Digby were bitter opponents, and Byron had long-standing grievances against Langdale. The King himself lacked the necessary strength of character to impose his will on his subordinates.

Whatever their reasons, the Royalist commanders in Chester were throwing away the opportunity for a decisive victory, and at the same time putting Langdale into increasing peril, for reaction in the enemy camp had been much more prompt.

Jones and Lothian possibly received news of Poyntz's reverse somewhat later than the King did, and the first reports were ominous:

it was noised that General Poyntz was utter Routed, which was sad news to our Forces in Chester, who upon consultation, at first thought fit to quit the Suburbs, lest, the Army miscarrying, all should be lost, but upon intelligence that Poyntz kept his ground and stood in a body, they resolved to keep what ground they had gotten for the gaining of Chester, and to assist General Poyntz with horse and foot, which he sent for and they promised...[13]

Soon after 2 p.m. the Cheshire Parliamentarians despatched southwards along the Whitchurch road a force of 350 horse under Lieutenant-General Michael Jones and a body of 400 musketeers led by Colonel John Booth. Their departure was marked by two cannon shots, a pre-arranged signal which raised 'a great shout' from Poyntz's men, still drawn up on Hatton Heath and eagerly awaiting assistance. The remainder of the Cheshire forces, about 1,000 foot and 150 horse, commanded by Major-General Lothian, were left to hold the captured suburbs: 'a work of great trust and courage.'[14]

The departure of the Cheshire troops was clearly visible from Chester, and a warning, possibly carried by the redoubtable Shakerley, was despatched to Langdale, who was instructed to withdraw nearer to Chester. In an attempt to obey, and also to avoid being trapped between Poyntz and the approaching Cheshire troops, Langdale shifted his position about a mile to the north-west on to Rowton Heath, a mixture of heathland and cultivated ground around the village of Rowton. But, possibly because threatened by the approach of the Cheshire forces, Langdale, unlike in his previous position, was unable to take full advantage of the terrain, and had to draw up entirely on the open ground.

Meanwhile the Royalist forces in Chester had at last begun to move:

[At] about four o'clock in the afternoon the Lord Gerrard marched out via the Northgate and made a long detour through the suburbs with the horse formerly mentioned (that is to say, the King's guard, his own Troop and the greatest part of the Horse I had drawn into the Town and five hundred foot.)[15]

The Royalist commander hoped to take Jones's force in the rear, but Lothian reacted by detaching 200 Shropshire horse under Lieutenant-Colonel Chidley Coote, probably all the cavalry he had left, formed into three divisions under Coote, Colonel Price and Major Fenwick, together with 200 Cheshire foot under Captain Daniell.

With a shorter distance to go, Coote intercepted Gerrard on Hoole Heath, to the east of Chester, and a confused engagement followed. Lord Digby claimed that the Parliamentarians were routed 'and driven back into their workes',[16] and it may have been at this point that Lord Bernard Stuart, the King's cousin and commander of his lifeguard of horse, 'charging with too much gallantry (near the suburbs where the Enemy lay entrenched) was there unfortunately slain.'[17] The Parliamentarian version was that Gerrard was routed, but, whatever the circumstances, it is clear that the Royalist force was at least held in check and prevented from either attacking Jones or joining Langdale.

By now, action was about to commence on Rowton Heath. The position here now was that Jones and Booth had linked up with Poyntz in the face of the Royalists, and a Parliamentarian army of just over 3,000 horse and 500 foot, the Cheshire element fairly fresh, were matched against Langdale's tired force of about 3,000 men.

Fighting began at about 4 p.m., when Poyntz,

> with a party advanced to take the most convenient ground, giving command to Colonel Parsons, Quartermaster-General of the Army… to order up the rest, which was opportunely done, for they joined with

50. Cavalry action (from John Vernon, *The Young Horseman*, 1644) Leading ranks are discharging their pistols; the body in the centre under attack from front and flank is collapsing.

the Auxiliary force of horse and foote in the enemyes ground and was drawne into many small divisions and reserves.[18]

The nature of the Parliamentarian deployment was probably dictated by the enclosed ground on the edge of Rowton village, where hedges and ditches hindered the horse. Booth's musketeers were drawn up in two bodies in the 'outermost intervals of the horse' though the bulk of Poyntz's cavalry were left under Parsons to act as a reserve.

The advance was commenced by the Cheshire horse, covered by the musketeers firing 'a round volley of shot.'

Langdale's men were drawn up on the open ground, possibly with Sir William Vaughan's and Gerrard's brigades, and Langdale's 'reformadoes' forming the first line, and the bulk of the Northern Horse in reserve. The Royalists advanced to meet the enemy attack, but at some stage seem to have been overlapped by some of the Parliamentarians, who 'charged them in front and flank.'[19]

A fierce struggle followed; the Royalists:

had the Wind and Sun, we had God with us, which was our word, counterpoising all disadvantages, and countermanding all strength. A little before five o'clock, we joined in a terrible storm, firing in the faces of one another, hacking and slashing with swords, neither party gained or lost a foot of ground, as if everyone were there resolved to breathe their laste.[20]

As the fighting continued, 'hot and doubtful', a key role was played by the Cheshire musketeers. Their threat may have already disrupted the Royalist advance, allowing Langdale's first line to be outflanked, and Booth's men now seem to have moved under cover of the enclosures around the flanks of Langdale's first line, and 'so galled their horse, that their Rear fled, perceiving their losse by them, upon whom they made no Execution.'[21] Digby wrote:

1,000 foot coming to them in the nick of time from the Lancashire [sic] side, they again pres'd upon us so fast, that our horse not being able to retreat to Chester, there to join with our other forces, they were fain to charge; which Sir William Vaughan's and General Gerrard's and Sir Marmaduke Langdale's Reformadoes did successfully enough, till the reserve of the Northern Horse, (just as they did at Naseby) took a fright before any enemy was near them, and ran.

Whereupon all our horse were put to great disorder and forc'd to disperse.[22]

The historian of the Cheshire Army claimed that:

the greatest burden lay upon the Cheshire Horse, because they were fresh for service, the rest being very much wearied with an incessant march and long fasting. Collonel Jones encouraged his souldiers with such language, that he drew teares from their eyes, and vowes from their mouthes, that they would stick fast to him, whether in life or death, which they faithfully performed. The rest also buckled themselves to the service in hand, and to give both sides Their due, they performed their work with as much vigour and resolution as could be expected from men.[23]

Another Parliamentarian account adds further details:

we hastened towards them in the best posture we could, the Horse was the Battel [centre], because many, the Wings were foot, because few... whilst the dispute was so hot and doubtful, our musquetiers so galled their horse, that their rear fled... Their Van, perceiving that, faced about and fled also; we had nothing to do, but to pursue and make execution, which we did to purpose, for though the ways were strewed with Arms, Portmantles, Cloakbags and Horse, we left those to any that would pillage, and fell to Execution...[24]

Some of the Royalists seem to have fled back into Wales via Holt Bridge, but most of them made for Chester, apparently becoming entangled with some of Gerrard's men.

These were composed of those, who following Collonel Jones, in the reere, were driven towards Bridge Trafford, and then escaped in the field, who were partly twisted in the Parliament Armie, while they pursued the victory, and part of them driven before us. Opportunity serving, they separated themselves, drew into a body, fell upon our pursuing Army, who suspected no danger, got ground of us, and put us to retreate...[25]

Disentangling this confused account, it seems that Langdale's men, reinforced by part of Gerrard's force, who had at last come up, launched an initially successful counterattack. This is confirmed by another account, which states that the Royalists had rallied, possibly on Hoole Heath,

> in two vaste bodies a great distance asunder… after we thought the worke was ended, the enemy made head again, and they that escaped in the field and about Chester, joined in another, fell upon part of our forces with advantage (for they were desperate seeing that they had lost the day) drove them to our mud walls…[26]

Parsons wrote that Langdale's troops:

> retreated [sic] upon the Warwick Regiment with such violence as bore them away confusedly, intermixed with the flying enemy, up to the outworks of the suburbs…[27]

But the Parliamentarians had the advantage of numbers, and 'more forces coming up, we drove them under the walls of the suburbs', from which Lothian's musketeers fired indiscriminately on the confused mass of horsemen.

The bulk of the Royalists were forced away to the north, where they became broken up and scattered among the narrow lanes and enclosed areas. Some, lacking local knowledge, were entangled in the ditches and marshes of the Gowey valley, where the Cheshire Parliamentarians captured sixty men and 100 horses. Others were drowned in the Gowey itself, or fled across it to seek refuge in Delamere Forest. The bulk however retreated into North Wales, or back into Chester itself, where the garrison, in an attempt to distract Lothian's men, had launched a sortie which was easily repulsed.

A last remaining organised body of Royalist horse (said by the Parliamentarians to include the King himself, though Charles had actually watched the closing stages of the battle from the tower of the cathedral and the Phoenix Tower) was drawn up on some higher ground in the Hoole Heath area, and Bethell and Lydcott's regiments of horse, with some Cheshire foot, were drawn up to face them. However, as dusk fell, the Royalists withdrew into Chester and fighting came to an end.

Rowton Heath was a major disaster for King Charles. Royalist casualties were variously estimated, and seem to have included about 600 dead, and a claimed 900 prisoners, although extant lists do not support such a total, which seems exaggerated.[28] To King Charles the greatest loss was the death of his cousin, the Earl of Lichfield, about fifty of whose lifeguard unit were also among the casualties, including the musician William Lawes, who was

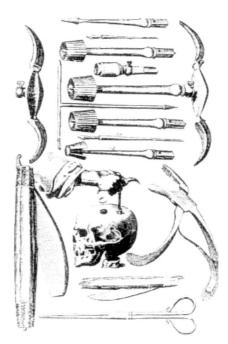

51. Medical instruments. Many instruments and surgical techniques were not dissimilar to their modern counterparts. Many of the instruments shown here were for use in trepanning operations.

probably serving as a volunteer with the lifeguard when he was killed in the fighting. Important prisoners of war included Major-General Sir Phillip Musgrave, Sir Henry Stradling and Colonel Thomas Dacres of the Northern Horse. Parliamentarian losses, though not stated, must also have been significant; both Bethell and Greaves were 'sore wounded', Colonel Price and Captain Culme were killed.

7

THE GREAT ASSAULT:
25 SEPTEMBER–8 OCTOBER 1645

Following the defeat of his army it was too dangerous for King Charles to remain in Chester, and on the morning of 25 September, accompanied by 500 horse, the disconsolate King rode out again over the Dee Bridge, his departure hidden from enemy eyes by a screen of hides, to take refuge at Denbigh while he considered his next move. During the next few days the Royalists rallied about 2,400 horse, but although Langdale's forces were within 2 miles of Holt no attempt was made to engage the enemy again.

The battle of Rowton Heath had, however, given the hard-pressed defenders of Chester a temporary respite. Enemy pressure on the town had slackened, as Poyntz and the Cheshire forces needed time to re-organise. But to Byron any advantage gained was not immediately apparent. The King's forces, during 'the two nights which they had spent in the town, had spent as much provision as would have sustained the whole garrison above a month, and [left] me in a desperate condition.'[1] The King, before leaving, had given Byron an opportunity to resign his command, and had given the citizens leave to seek terms if he was unable to keep the Welsh side of the city open.

Byron described the situation now facing him:

No Public Magazine of Victual and at such a time of the year when the old store was spent and the new but coming in. Seventeen thousand mouths at the least to feed, who would not be regulated in their diet, because they had their provisions in their own custody. A Regiment of Burghers only to rely upon, and many of these suspected persons, and about a hundred Irish under the command of Lieutenant Colonel Little, only Colonel Mostyn had brought in part of his Flintshire Regiment consisting of two hundred men, who had formerly been soldiers, and Sir Edmund Verney, the day before the King went, marched in with five hundred men of Colonel Hugh Gwinn's [Wynne's] Regiment, who hardly knew the use of their arms. The Town Regiment (under the command of Sir Francis Gamull) was eight hundred strong all those musketeers excepting one hundred and for their supplies, as well as for the cannon (whereof there were eleven pieces mounted) and all other uses (as hand granadoes fireworks and the like) but seven barrels of powder and a half with match hardly proportionable.[2]

Byron's problems were increased by the inevitable drop in morale which followed the Royalist defeat and the King's departure, which,

together with the impossibility in all mens' opinions that it could be kept for any time, caused many Gentlemen and Reformadoes to lay hold of that opportunity to leave the Town, so that it was left very naked for the present, till afterwards it was replenished with such as had made their escapes from the fight, and having lost their horses, could not follow his Majesty, amongst which a French Gentleman, (who gave himself the name of Lord St Paul [St Pol]) was one. The same day likewise Colonel Wate [Henry Waite] (a well-experienced officer) came to me out of Wales, and kept a constant Post in the Town until the end of the siege.[3]

Byron had now to concert measures to make best use of the resources available to him.

In the first place I called the Officers, the Mayor of the City and the Commissioners of Array together and advised with them what was fittest to be done to defend ourselves till it should please God to send us relief. And in order to that, propounded many things to them. First, that a Public Magazine should be made for Victuals and officers appointed to dispense it with order and proportion to the Soldiers: but that the Mayor answered could not be done without danger of a mutiny the stores of Corns being in private hands and many of them soldiers of the Garrison, who would not suffer it to be in any custody but their own. – The next proposition was that a sum of money should be raised for setting forward the powder-work: payment of the Welsh soldiers, and doing other necessary works for the strength of the Town; to which a great willing-ness was pretended by the Mayor; but an absolute disability of raising any considerable sum, in regard of the poverty of the City for want of trade. The Gentry residing in the City were willing but (by reason they had been so long debarred from any profit out of their estates, possessed wholly by the Rebels) were able to do little only for the present; it was ordered that the two Welsh regiments should have a proportion of bread allowed them daily which after a while was turned into threepence a day in money and they to find themselves. And of all the money collected both for that and other public services, the Mayor himself was both Steward and Paymaster. As for their lodging (though the weather was extremely cold) they had no other than what a great school house afforded them, and hardly straw enough to lie upon, in regard the Town was pestered with so many people that fled out of the Suburbs upon the Enemy's surprisal of them. To Officers, there was not anything allowed, save only free quarter. As for the providing of powder and match something was promised, but little done, but what I was forced to lay out of my own purse. Order was likewise taken for the setting of the guards, the officers assigned their several posts, and patrols of horse appointed for the Streets, and a guard of horse near unto Newgate, where the breach was made, and the duty changed from every third to every second night. The Earl of Lemster, the Lord Viscount Kilmorrey, and the rest of the Gentlemen to take their turns at watching every other night at the penthouse where we kept our main guard, myself to be with them one night, and the Lieutenant Governor Sir Francis Gamull another, to watch the rounds and see that the Soldiers and Officers passed upon their duty and be ready to prevent any mutiny or treachery which I was more doubtful might happen within the Town, than of anything the Enemy could do without.[4]

The fate of the King's cousin, the Earl of Lichfield, killed in the battle, had not been known for certain when Charles left Chester, but on the 26 September Colonel John Booth sent word to Byron that a body believed to be Lichfield's had been found, and on this being confirmed, Booth (rejecting, according to Byron, a 'barbarous' suggestion from some of his fellow officers that it be held for ransom),

with great civility brought the Corpse with a guard of foot and forty horse to a place agreed upon betwixt us, without the walls of the city, where I

52. The exchange. It was not unusual for the bodies of notables which fell into enemy hands after a battle to be handed over to their own side or to relatives. It was also not unknown for some kind of payment to be demanded in return.

met it, with such Noblemen and Gentlemen as were in the garrison, and an equal number of horse and so conveyed it into the City.[5]

Here the body was embalmed and kept until after the siege, when it was sent to Oxford for burial. This incident of civility did not halt military operations; on the same day Lord Digby, with the King at Denbigh, wrote in an endeavour to encourage Byron.

His Majesty is very well pleased with the resolution expressed by the town of Chester and sends them herewithal a letter of thanks. Here is now with his Majesty the Archbishop of York, Sir John Owen and diverse others with whom he has taken the best order he can for the supply of Chester with provisions, viz butter, cheese and cattle out of those countries, as also corn out of these. The King likewise resolves to send Sir William Blakiston to you in Chester with a good proportion of horse, and to have a considerable body under Sir W. Vaughan for the keeping of the Welsh side open. I beseech you encourage the town all you can, for I do not despair but we may ere long find means to ease you of your ill neighbours.[6]

Byron was probably not greatly comforted by these promises; he would have been hard put to have fed Blakiston's men and horses if they had arrived, and may have said so, as the troops were never sent. Digby expressed some of his fears in a letter sent the same day to Ormonde:

> This enclosed relation will let you see the danger of Chester, which is somewhat more than is here expressed, through want of powder. You are conjured to hasten over some supply thither of ammunition and if possible of men. You know the importance of that place in relation to Ireland.[7]

Poyntz, probably because of the need to reorganise his own forces, had not immediately followed up the victory at Rowton Heath. However on 27 September he was back in action. At 5 p.m. that evening an apprehensive Byron wrote to Digby:

> At this instant all the enemy's horse appear before the town on the Cheshire side, tomorrow, as one who comes from amongst them assures me, Poyntz passes over into Wales; so that unless the King's horse be very active in beating up their quarters and cutting off provisions from the enemy this town will speedily be enforced to a parley. The same party who comes from amongst them speaks of the great joy they express for a late victory over Montrose, whereof they are so confident that they have shot off their cannon at Nantwich and other garrisons. I do not like this return of Poyntz's horse. I fear something is amiss with my Lord of Montrose. All that can be done for the present is that the King raise the whole force of Wales and command the horse immediately to advance this way, to straiten them in their quarters, and to procure good order.[8]

Byron was correct in his forebodings; Montrose had suffered a decisive defeat on 13 September at Philliphaugh. Early on 28 September Poyntz and his horse crossed the Wirral fords into Wales. The King's forces made no attempt to intervene, but retreated back into England by way of Chirk, heading on eastwards by way of Bridgenorth to Newark, from where Digby wrote with typically misplaced optimism to Byron hoping that the move would have drawn Poyntz away from Chester, and promising that Sir William Vaughan's brigade would be sent back to clear Chester's communications with Wales: 'God send that you may hold out till they come.'[9]

Poyntz, whilst retaining pursuit of the King as his main objective, was authorised by Parliament to provide assistance for a limited period in completing the capture of Chester. The next few days witnessed a quickening in the pace of Parliamentarian operations. Their artillery resumed its bombardment, and on 27 September Randle Holme noted:

> for a Sabbeth preparation they lett fly fourteen of their great shott at the Eastgate – they employed these to seek a reformation upon it and bring it low and uniform with their neighbour walls, but to small purpose, for tho they slew one for his too high aspirations, yet they cannot beat her into humility.
>
> On Sunday they startled our devotions with their continued volleyes, disturbing those whom they saw about to go to the house of God, sending in their messengers of mortality through the windows as if it were to forbid them the use of that place, but belike their aime is to drive out the service book which makes them handle the church so roughly…[10]

On 29 September the garrison received reports of a plan to mine the walls by digging tunnels and planting charges of gunpowder beneath them, to 'prevent which we countermyne for severall dayes together, and like moles prepare to meet their miners.'[11] The besiegers were also preparing a new battery in the vicinity of St John's Church, as well as moving troops to the Welsh side of the Dee in order to intensify the blockade. Byron wrote:

> they likewise began to pass a bridge of boats over the river under the Earl of Darbye's garden (for the better communication of their quarters one with another, and not thinking it safe at that time of the year to attend upon the uncertainties of the fords) though I gave what interruption I could by frequent sallies from the Fort of Handbridge (where Lieutenant-Colonel Robinson, a very active and intelligent man commanded) and thereby retarded their work but could I not absolutely hinder them from perfecting it. I endeavoured also (upon the prejudice I found from the musketeers they had placed upon St John's Steeple which overlooked all the Town) to beat it down but having only one piece of battery and that but a twelve-pounder, and finding that it would cause the expense of more powder than I could well spare was forced to give it over.[12]

The Parliamentarians were intensifying their attack:

> to hasten the work of reducing the City, we sent a convoy for the great guns at Stafford and [Shrewsbury] by them to force a speedie entrie,

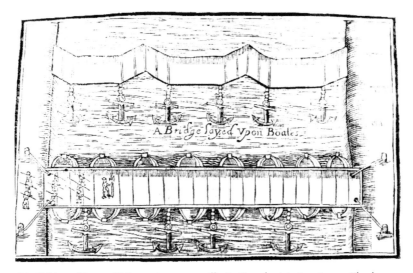

53. Bridge of boats. This contemporary illustration depicts two types. The lower example is probably the kind of bridge constructed by the Parliamentarians at Chester.

before the King could reinforce himselfe to returne, Powder and Ball was altogether wanting for so great a service, but the Gentlemen of the County were so forward for the worke, that they engaged themselves for four hundred pounds, by which we were furnished with Ammunition from Warrington; but such juggling there was to prevent the ball, and retard the guns, and by subtill agents, that cannot endure the work should prosper in the hands of those instruments (who affect the cause, as they fancie the Leader) that we lost above a weeke for the affecting of this great Designe.[13]

These criticisms were presumably aimed at Sir William Brereton, whom the writer, the Presbyterian clergyman Nathaniel Lancaster, disliked on religious grounds. He suggests that Brereton's supporters in Cheshire were attempting to hinder operations against Chester until Sir William could resume command.

The artillery included 'a great brasse piece of Ordnance', probably a whole cannon, and three other guns, but while their battery was being prepared, the besiegers' existing ordnance continued to batter Chester. On 4 October twenty-four cannon shots were aimed at the old breach near the Newgate, and, after firing two or three shots in reply, the Royalist twelve-pounder was dismounted by a 30lb shot. The breach was repaired by the townsfolk, after which there was a comparative lull for two days, during which the attackers continued to tighten their grip on the Welsh side.[14]

The Royalists made the best use they could of the breathing space. Byron watched as the enemy:

drew men into the Northgate suburbs, which were not so demolished but that they afford them shelter. From thence they drew four pieces of cannon, and raised a battery against that part of the wall called the Goblin's Tower and drew two other small pieces over the ford to another place on the Welsh side, called Brewershall, from whence they flancked all that part of the wall on the inside, so that had I not in some measure prevented it by making blinds it had not been possible to stand to defend the line. Another battery of two pieces they raised near to the New Gate (the place where they had made their first breach) by which preparations it was evident the Enemy intended another assault. Besides I had intelligence of a great proportion of scaling ladders that were made for that purpose. The wall of the City (the only fortification which was found generally to be weak upon experiences of the former breach so soon and so easily made). Whereupon (for the better encouragement of others) I had begun not long before with some Officers and Gentlemen to throw up a rampier [earth rampart] against the wall for the strengthening of it which afterwards by good example the Ladies and Gentlewomen gave in

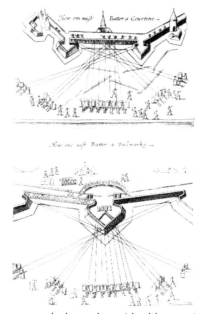

54. Battery Fire. Military manuals devoted considerable attention to the most effective employment of artillery in siege operations. These diagrams illustrate the recommended deployment of guns, with angles of fire, against different types of fortification.

55. Women in the breach. Chester's women played a major role in the efforts to fill the breaches before both of the major Parliamentarian assaults, suffering a number of casualties. Particularly before the October attack they were partly motivated by fear of their fate in the event of the enemy succeeding in taking the city.

their own persons, by carrying earth themselves to the works and the Mayor's diligence was in a short time brought to so good effect that the weakest parts of the wall were in most places very well secured.[15]

Some of the breaches and weak points were strengthened and filled up with beds and woolpacks, as entries in the town records describe:

1645 3 October: Ordered that one half of the beddes, wooll packs and other necessaries provided for the making upp of Breaches be forthwith carried to St Bridget's Church into some house near there, and the other halfe to bee putt into the house of Alderman Harveye neare the Breach.

1645 6 October: Order to Alderman Holme to take from the Glovers such coarse wool as they had to be made into packs, and employed in filling up the Breaches.[16]

By 8 October Sydenham Poyntz regarded his preparations as complete, but before launching his assault he followed military custom, and summoned Chester to surrender.

Sir,

Although our condition be such that we need not court you (and notwithstanding your scornful rejection of former summons) to clear our innocence before God and men of desiring the effusion of Christian blood, or the ruin of that ancient city, we once more demand the same with the Castle and Fort for the use of King and Parliament, upon such conditions as may be honourable to both parties: which offer not embraced, and your acceptance thereof not signified to us within this hour, what miseries shall ensue by fire, sword and spoil, from enraged Soldiers, let be charged upon your head, and let the world witness our unwillingness to use extremities if you constrain not,

Your Servants

Sydenham Poyntz

Mic. Jones

James Lothian

8th 8bris 1645

For the Lord Byron.[17]

Byron, whose main aim was to gain as much time as possible to complete his preparations, consulted with his officers and the city authorities, then replied:

Gentlemen,

Your letter of Summons intimating a former letter to the same purpose (which neither came to our hands or knowledge) we have received; to which we return you this answer; that we neither apprehend your condition to be so high, nor ours (God be thanked) so low as to be threatened out of this City, and that we have received his Majesty's express command for the keeping thereof: and cannot without his knowledge, break so great a trust laid upon us. And therefore must require liberty of fourteen days, to give his Majesty an account of your demands and to receive his further pleasure. To which purpose, we shall appoint a Gentleman and a Citizen for whom we shall desire a free pass, forthwith to his Majesty and to return to us without let or interruption, and to have the conduct of a Trumpet of yours. At the expiration of which time we will hearken to a Treaty upon honourable conditions for the City, Castle and Fort, if his Majesty do not relieve us. And in the meantime shall expect that a Cessation of Arms and working, shall be punctually upon honour observed on both sides. If you shall refuse this customary and soldierly proceeding, we then do declare in the names of the Noblemen, Gentlemen, Citizens and Soldiers within this garrison, that we defy the fury of your enraged soldiers, and doubt not (with God's blessing) to defend and maintain this City for his Majesty and ourselves as it is now, against any assaults that shall be made with as much resolution and courage as formerly.

> Your Servants,
> John Byron
> Charles Walley Mayor
> 8th 8bris 1645.[18]

Byron took care to ensure that Walley's signature appeared alongside his, on both this and subsequent communications:

> both the more to engage him, and to the end our good agreement and consent in the defence of the City (the greatest part of the garrison consisting of Citizens) might the better appear.[19]

As Byron no doubt expected, Poyntz and his fellow commanders next day rejected his proposals, warning him that if he refused to open negotiations, 'you must expect what you defy, the fury of enraged soldiers', and demanding his response within half an hour.

Byron:

> gladly received this answer, having formerly engaged the Mayor and his bretheren in case of such a refusal, not to admit of any Treaty, but to join with me in the defence of the City to the uttermost.[20]

He assured the citizens that the enemy would only have rejected his 'reasonable' requests if they knew that the King was already marching to Chester's relief, and rejected the Parliamentarians' demands, warning them that 'We are therefore ready to defend ourselves to the utmost of your rage, not doubting of God's blessing and protection…'[21]

Poyntz did not wait for the promised half hour's grace to elapse before resuming hostilities. On the previous day his guns at Brewershall had opened fire against the Northgate, and musketeers entrenched on the Welsh bank of the Dee or other nearby high ground had been able to outflank the defending fortifications, causing some annoyance, though the Royalists claimed that the enemy bombardment had succeeded only in uprooting 'an old tree'.

When the main cannonade began, late on the morning of 9 October, the Parliamentarians scored an early success when they dismounted a small Royalist gun stationed on the Goblin Tower. Their main effort was directed against the wall between the Goblin Tower and the Northgate, firing coming from a battery in the northern suburbs and from the Brewershall position. The bombardment was heavy; 'near 400 great shot' according to Byron, whilst with a precision difficult to believe, Holme reckoned the total to be '357 of their tennis balls.' Estimates of the damage caused differ; Lancaster wrote that the wall:

> proved so thicke, and the Ball so brittle, that not much more than the battlements was beaten downe; whilst the besieged endeavoured to make up the breach by packs, feather-beds etc and to lyne the Wall all along; our Cannon on the Welsh side made great execution, swords, armes, legges, whole bodies were seene to fly in the ayre, cart loads of bodies drawne off, and the Horse in the reare driving up men and women to make up the breach.[22]

Randle Holme merely commented that the loss was 'not great', whilst Byron reported that:

> A breach was made near the Goblin's Tower; but not easy to be assaulted by reason of a dry ditch under the wall, which they were to pass before they came to the breach. Their other battery near the Newgate, made not that effect they expected by reason of the rampier newly cast up which had made the wall Cannon-proof.[23]

The Royalists stood to arms in expectation of an imminent assault, knowing that the fate of city and citizens if it succeeded was likely to be grim indeed. At the north breach Colonel Vane was in command, with Captain Gethin's company of Wynne's regiment and Captain Norris and Lieutenant Lane of Byron's foot. In the New Tower was Captain Henry Lloyd of Wynne's regiment and Lieutenant King, whilst held in reserve were the companies of Captain Goulbourne (possibly one of the reformadoes who had come in after Rowton Heath) and Captain Thomas Price of Roger Mostyn's regiment.[24]

A little before sunset, probably at about 4 p.m., despite the incomplete success of their bombardment, the Parliamentarians:

> began to storm the Town at both Breaches, and to scale the walls on all parts (but upon the Rood-eye, where the river hindered them) with

56. Morgan's Mount. This gun platform on the city walls was probably constructed during the war. The actual 'Morgan's Mount' was part of the outworks just below this section of the walls.

great resolution. At the breach (near Goblin's Tower which afterwards went by the name of the new breach) Colonel George Vane commanded, and Sir Edmund Verney at the Newgate, which we called the old breach. These two Gentlemen, during the whole Siege, through their extraordinary care and diligence, were a great help to me. To Monsieur St Paul, I gave the command of the horse that day, which he discharged with much honour and gallantry. Myself, with some Gentlemen with me, rode about the walls continually, from one guard to another, both to encourage the soldiers, and see such things supplied as were wanting in any place. The enemy stormed the new breach with great disadvantage, having both a very steep bank to ascend, and when they were got up, a precipice to come down, and withal were flanked by two towers, (the Goblin's Tower on the one hand and the New Tower on the other) from whence our musketeers were not sparing of their shot. Notwithstanding all such disadvantages they both assaulted it and brought their ladders to the wall, and began to scale with a great fury. The line was filled with halberdiers where I had likewise caused heaps of stones to be laid in convenient distances, which when the Enemy came under the walls, did more execution than muskets could have done, the shot was placed upon the flankers of the wall, where it was most useful. Our men for a good space were at handy blows with them

57. Storming a breach. Success in storming a defensive position depended upon a number of factors. It was preferable to launch assaults simultaneously at several locations against weak points in the defences or 'assaultable' breaches. Here a dense column of troops is attempting to overwhelm defenders by weight of numbers. Note the large number of hand 'granadoes' being used.

on top of the wall. The Enemy (as fast as their ladders were thrown down and their men knocked off) rearing up others in their stead, and bringing up fresh supplies…[25]

It was probably in the course of this fierce struggle that:

my Lorde St Paule (almost as naked as his sword) ran rageinge in his shirt, up to the North Breach, where the enemy prest extremely for an entrance, but were by him so bravely back't that sudden death denies them tyme to call for quarter. Others who escaped the like condition were glad to use their heels.[26]

St Pol's state of undress was probably the result of stripping to his shirt for ease of recognition by his own men in the gathering dusk.

At the same time the Storm was begun in all other places, but at the Newgate (where Sir Edmund Verney commanded) continued not long, the breach there not being assaultable, and the wall too high for their ladders. So that, (finding a few men would defend that place) I drew the greatest part of them to the Phoenix and Saddler's Towers, being but low and without any ditch, and the approach secured by walls and houses, within less than Carbine shot of the walls of the City, so that there the business was very hotly disputed. But at length, it pleased God both there and in all places they were beaten off, and forced to leave their ladders behind them, whereof a great number with a good proportion of arms were brought into the Town. The days were then short and the darkness of the night saved many of their lives. At the same time, they intended to have attempted something upon the Fort at Handbridge, where three or four hundred of Poyntz his troops dismounted, and with their swords and pistols in their hands, marched towards the Fort (where Lieutenant Colonel Robinson commanded) as if they proposed to have stormed it, but by the time they came within musket shot of it, liked it so ill, that they retreated without doing anything. I must not forget the great courage and gallantry the Chester women expressed that day, who all the time the cannon played upon the new breach (whereof two were whole Culverin, and the other two pieces of 36 pound ball, besides these smaller pieces, that flanked the breach from Brewer's Hall),… carried both Earth and feather beds, and other materials incessantly, and made up the breach in the very mouth of the cannon. And though 8 or ten of them at the least, were killed and spoiled with great shot, yet the rest were nothing at all dismayed, but followed on their work, with as great alacrity and as little fear as if they had been going to milk their cows.[27]

Randle Holme also wrote with admiration of the role of the Chester women:

By this tyme our women are all on fire, striving through a gallant emulation to outdoe our men and will make good our yielding walls or lose their lives. Seven are shot and three slain, yet they scorn to leave their undertaking, and this they continue for ten days space. Our ladies likewise like so many exemplary goddesses create a matchlesse forward-ness in the meaner sort by their durtye undertakings.[28]

After two hours of fighting the Parliamentarian attacks had been everywhere repulsed. Losses, particularly among the attackers, are difficult to estimate. The Parliamentarians themselves admitted to at most twenty-seven dead, including a sergeant and a corporal, and between sixty and eighty wounded, among them Lieutenant-Colonel Venables, wounded in the arm, and Captain Massey, brother to the former governor of Gloucester.[29] Byron felt that enemy losses were heavy, but:

> What men the Enemy lost, I could not learn, they having ever had an extraordinary art in the concealing of their losses; but I am sure it could not but be great, all the Villages in that part of the Country being filled with their wounded men, besides those we saw lie dead under the walls (who they had leave to carry off the next day) and a great number whom they had drawn off in the darkness of the night.[30]

One of the Parliamentarian wounded was William Kernison of Milton Green, who in 1647 petitioned the Cheshire quarter sessions for relief, claiming that he had served,

> at the last assault made by the Parliament forces against Chester, [when] your petitioner was twice cast off a scaling ladder… he was greviously wounded whereby hee was constrained to lye a long time under the Chyurgeon's hands and to have one of his great toes cut off.[31]

Royalist losses were much lighter; Byron reported that they totalled about forty including ten dead. The most notable of these were Sir William Mainwaring, major to Sir Francis Gamull, and another of his officers, Captain Adlington, mortally wounded on the walls near the Saddler's Tower.[32]

Byron paid tribute to the courage of the mayor and citizens, who:

> expressed as much loyalty as could be, wisely considering that had the Town been carried by assault little distinction would have been made betwixt friend and foe.[33]

This claim was certainly correct, but, although the Royalists had won an encouraging success, it remained to be seen how well morale would bear up in the face of the hardships of a prolonged siege.

8

TIGHTENING SIEGE:
OCTOBER–NOVEMBER 1645

Though the great Parliamentarian assault had been repulsed, Byron's assessment of his situation immediately afterwards gave him small comfort.

> The rebels being thus repulsed, and the citizens thereby much encouraged, I took an account of what ammunition was left, and found but two barrels of powder and a half, with match scarce proportionable in the same. This I kept as a great and sad secret to myself: for had either the storm continued any longer, or been renewed the next morning, as I was doubtful it might be… the very want of Ammunition must of necessity have delivered us into their hands. But it pleased God at that time otherwise to dispose of things, for neither had they the courage to attempt anything upon us again, nor had we (by reason of the great want of Ammunition) wherewithall to take advantage of their fears; only this benefit I reaped by it, that I had time to set the powder mills to work, and to get some small proportion of Ammunition beforehand, and for the supply of match, was able to make use of the oakham and old cordage of a ship and hardly make shift (by all the means that could be devised) to supply the ordinary expense of the guards, who every three days burnt a hundredweight.[1]

Byron also sent an urgent appeal for powder to Ormonde in Dublin, and during the next few weeks about twenty barrels were shipped over, easing the worst of his shortages.[2]

Despite his lack of ammunition, Byron harassed the besiegers with numerous small-scale sorties.

> The few horse I had in Town, which were not above a hundred (the rest being sent out for want of provisions to sustain them) almost every morning marched out of the Bridgegate (which was kept open during the whole Siege) to take advantage upon the Enemy, as they should find occasion, and sometimes fell into their quarters, whereby they obliged them to extraordinary hard duty...[3]

In one such raid, on 15 October, Captains Dutton and Crosby beat up enemy quarters in Eccleston, killing about thirty enemy foot, and bringing back as prisoners Captain Carter's lieutenant, Philomen Mainwaring, and four troopers, with the captain's trumpet and colours.[4]

Such successes further boosted the confidence of Chester's defenders, already encouraged by their victory on 9 October. Some idea of their mood at this time may be gleaned from a batch of letters written by some of the Welsh soldiers in the city which was intercepted by the Parliamentarians. On 16 October, one of the Welsh, Thomas Rogers, recounted rumours then current that Poyntz (who had now left the immediate vicinity of Chester) had been defeated by Sir William Vaughan, and that Montrose was marching south through Lancashire with 12,000 men to their assistance.[5] However on the same day a less optimistic viewpoint was presented by Rinald David, probably a soldier in Roger Mostyn's regiment, writing perhaps to the son of his employer:

> This is to understand that we are in good health, but I desire you or my wife to send me some money with this bearer or the first that cometh. For I do stand in great want, for there is nothing to be had here without money, and God knows our allowance is very small.[6]

His view was not echoed by another writer, Major Maurice Thelwall of Hugh Wynne's regiment, who told his wife:

> our soldiers are very well provided for; they have 2d a day paid to them and a pound of bread...[7]

Next day Hugh Wynne himself and several of his officers, in a letter perhaps intended mainly to raise morale among their soldiers' relatives, wrote:

we keep very good and constant guard, our men are very cheerful, and so be the townsmen, emulating one another who shall do the best service. The town is full of provision and we that are strangers want nothing so long as we have money. Here is as good 16d ordinary [a meal provided in an inn at a fixed price] as ever was in time of peace.[8]

A touching reminder of the traumatic effects of war on the lives of ordinary folk appears in another letter from the intercepted package, written at about the same time as the others. A Welsh woman, Mrs Walter Edwards, trapped in the city, writes to her husband, who had apparently been absent on business when the siege began:

I do not know what to do nor what to say, but I do not desire you here, not for all the world. But I desire myself with you with all my heart and soul, for God knows I have but small joy to be from you, but was God that would have it to be. So I desire God to grant you patience and not to lay it so much to heart as I know you do. For God's sake be as merry as you can, for I make no doubt that God will bring us together very shortly with joy. If you were here you must watch and ward as all men do. God in his mercy amend these times. Here is more killed looking on than those who are on service. You need not fear for me, for I am so fearful I go no whither out of door, and if any do well I hope I shall do well, for none of us is in fear God be thanked…[9]

With the failure of their great assault, and in any case lacking the manpower for another such attack after the departure of Poyntz, the besiegers prepared for a long haul. They had had problems in countering Royalist sorties because of difficulties in moving troops quickly from one bank of the Dee to the other (the nearest ford was at Boughton). On 18 October the bridge of boats was completed; it spanned the river at the bottom of Dee Lane, and would eventually be protected on the Welsh side by two mounts, the lower one (whose remains may still be traced) on the river bank, and the higher mount further up the hill in the modern Queen's Park.[10]

On 20 October the Parliamentarians scored a success of their own. Troops under Michael Jones were sent to Holt to disperse a Royalist force said to be 700 strong, which had gathered to relieve Beeston. Owing to a premature attack by their forlorn hope, the Parliamentarian attempt at a surprise failed, enabling the Royalist defenders of Holt Castle to close its gates in time, but the Parliamentarians fell on about 140 Royalist horse and some of the garrison foot:

58. Encounter with a bear. Raids aimed at rounding up livestock were an important means of disrupting Chester's supplies. The presence of the bear remains unexplained. It may have been kept by the garrison of Holt for amusements such as bear-baiting.

with such violence, that we beat them into the Castle ditch, made great execution on them in the fall, slew one Major, and many other soldiers, wounded very many, took Lieutenant-Colonel [William] Byron, the Lord Byron's brother, five more and some good horses; our losse was two men slaine, three wounded, not mortally, others slightly wounded, fourteene of our forlorne hope taken, whose neglect of commands rendered them prisoners.[11]

At about the same time, Major Jerome Zankey raided Hawarden, taking forty-two cattle, 590 sheep, fourteen horses and, rather to the consternation of all concerned, 'A Bear, which roared upon the man that layd hold on him for a calfe.' To the townsfolk offering to pay contributions to the Parliamentarians, livestock was restored, though the fate of the bear is unrecorded.[12]

The next few days were relatively quiet, though two of the garrison of Chester were killed by sniper fire. The Parliamentarians had by now moved two of their guns to a position on the bowling green south of St John's Church, from where they began to bombard the Dee Mills near the Bridgegate and the water tower mounted on the latter.

Randle Holme gave a detailed description of the bombardment:

thirteen great shot are forthwith made which do little hurt save the cutting off of two of our men. And now a long boat comes up the river and salutes us with two piece of cannon and the night following with three more, for since they can do no good by land, they will at least make us laugh by sea and smile to see their folly.[13]

On the 25 October, Holme claimed, the Parliamentarian guns aimed seventeen shots at the water tower. One of these, presumably an incendiary, set fire to a gorse stack, and the flames spread to two adjacent houses, but 'our men like so many salamanders seem to take it up, for otherwise we scarce know how it was so suddenly extinguished.'[14] Next day the besiegers fired sixteen shots, and the water pipes leading from the tower were temporarily severed.

During the night a cannon shot took off the leg of a miller:

but this is nothing to their masterpiece. A great granado [incendiary shell] guarded with four light matches slept in a wooden basin, comes down the water, and is designed to fire the mills, but being discovered by the sentinels was stifled at the water before its time of execution.[15]

The bombardment continued, without notable effect, over the next two days. The overall effect of these cannonades, which continued spasmodically into

59. View of Chester from Welsh side of the Dee. Following the failure of their second assault the besiegers directed spasmodic artillery fire against the city walls and riverside mills in this sector. The royalist 'mount' on high ground near Handbridge prevented them approaching the Welsh end of the Dee Bridge.

December, were to leave three of the five mills severely damaged, and inflicted a good deal of other incidental damage in the process. Marks left by projectiles fired during these attacks may still be seen on Barnaby's Tower, near the south-eastern angle of the walls.[16]

Meanwhile, Chester's most implacable foe, Sir William Brereton, restored by Parliament to his old command, was about to resume charge of operations. Byron was typically scathing about his return:

> Sir William Brereton (upon petition from the Zealots of that County) was called down to reap the honour of other mens' actions. Matter of danger, (which Sir Will. Brereton never greatly loved) was then pretty well past; and the King having no Army in the field, nor likely to have any in haste: industry and patience he knew (wherein few excel him) must in time carry that City which had ever been his chiefest aim.[17]

Brereton's main concern as he rode north were reports of an imminent attempt by Sir William Vaughan, 'the Devil of Shrawardine' to relieve Chester. Michael Jones was confident that the besiegers could hold some of their siegeworks as self-contained forts, and draw off their guns to the safety of Tarvin, for long enough to see off any relief force.[18]

60. Sir William Brereton. An alternative image from the 'heroic' pose of Illustration 5. Byron was not alone in alleging cowardice by Sir William, similar accusations also being levelled by fellow Parliamentarians. There is, however, no direct evidence to support them.

On 26 October the Cheshire militia were called out to release some of the front-line troops at Chester to meet the threat from Vaughan. However this resulted in a financial crisis which greeted Brereton on his arrival on 27 October.

> At my coming to the Leaguer I had no sooner dismounted at Tarvin but I was mett with complaints from Jones and Lothian of a very hot meeting amongst the soldiers for want of pay alleging the arrears of very neere two months of pay.[19]

Brereton managed to quiet the immediate crisis, although the problem would recur. He now felt the time to be ripe to try the effects of propaganda on the citizens, and fired into Chester a number of arrows carrying messages urging the defenders to submit:

> love letters, stuff full of such fair promises as they think will ravish our resolves into a tame submission – we send back their shafts with an answer made of wildfire – that they might see by their houses how hot our love was to them, for they flamed extremely…[20]

Byron was equally dismissive of Brereton's efforts; the letters contained, he said:

> many specious arguments to move the citizens to mutiny and rebellion, but at that time their ears were stopped against his charms, charmed he never so wisely.[21]

The citizens were influenced partly by hopes of imminent relief by Vaughan, and even more by fears of the vengeance which Brereton would wreak if he captured Chester. These apprehensions did much to stiffen their resolve, though significantly in the mayoral elections of October the relatively moderate Charles Walley was re-elected in preference to a more extreme Royalist.

The attention of both sides was now focusing on the activities of Sir William Vaughan. A sixty-year-old, hard-bitten professional soldier, Vaughan had been entrusted by the King with the task of keeping open supply routes into Chester. Unfortunately, though, even after stripping remaining Royalist garrisons in the area of all available men, Vaughan could muster only 1,500 horse and foot, an insufficient force, even with the equivocal assistance of the North Wales Royalists, to dislodge the besieging army of up to 5,000 men. Reports of Vaughan's march northwards along the Welsh Border caused a flurry of alarm among the Parliamentarian commanders at Chester, Jones warning that 'the whole kingdom depends upon this bout…'[22]

This was a considerable exaggeration, especially as James Lothian on 27 October told Brereton that he could draw off 1,500 men from the siege lines to reinforce troops under Michael Jones on the Welsh side of the Dee. By the end of 29 October, Vaughan, with 1,200 horse and 300 foot, mostly poorly armed, was quartered at Ruabon, moving next day to Denbigh. On 31 October Jones and Lothian, with 1,200 horse and 1,500 foot, set off in search of Vaughan.[23]

Early on 1 November the Parliamentarians came up with Vaughan, who was taken partly by surprise, near the village of Whitchurch, about a mile east of Denbigh. After some preliminary skirmishing between opposing musketeers among the hedgerows, the Royalist horse, hastily drawn up on Denbigh Green, broke and fled with little resistance.

On 4 November, Vaughan rallied his forces at Llanrwst, and found that he still mustered 800 horse and 250 foot. But what little enthusiasm he had ever had for his hopeless mission had now evaporated, and, retreating through central Wales, by 12 November Vaughan's men had dispersed back to their garrisons. Relief for Royalist Chester seemed more remote than ever.[24]

In the city conditions had begun to worsen, bringing with them the first trickle of deserters. On the same day that Vaughan was defeated, three Royalist deserters – a sergeant, a drummer and a common soldier – had themselves lowered by ropes from the walls by a gunner, to whom they had promised a share in some hidden valuables which they claimed to be going to recover. Brought before Parliamentarian officers, they painted a gloomy picture of conditions in Chester.

> three mills and the water pipe spoiled, no scarcity of victuals yet but among the Welsh, who beg all their meat and are almost famished, and both soldiers and citizens in daily discontent.[25]

In an effort to maintain morale, letters were read out at every parade, purporting to relate various Parliamentarian defeats.

A flurry of action came on 3 November. Possibly distracted by news of the victory at Denbigh Green, some of the Parliamentarian outposts relaxed their vigilance, and this was combined with the return of some of the victorious troops, mistaken by the Royalists for beaten fugitives.

> whereupon my Lord St Paul sallys with a party of horse and foot, Lieutenant Harrison hath the van, and advance behind the river unto

the Welsh side where the enemy lay. He charges on – the enemy run – he follows till at last he is presented with the body of an approaching army. 200 fresh foot now combine with our party to draw up in a body to face the enemy, which they perceiving, send us two piece of cannon, and these are doubled six times over, during the skirmish. The enemy outman us with their multitudes, yet after a long encounter our retreat is honourable, having no more harme done save two slain and three shot. The enemy lost thirty at least, besides five prisoners. Our reserve of foot consisted most of Welshmen commanded by Col. Roger Mostyn, and his officers leave their commendation to the enemy, whose blood proclaims them gallant.[26]

In what Nathaniel Lancaster said was 'a very sharp skirmish of long continu-ance', Brereton admitted only to losing three or four dead, the same number wounded, and five or six prisoners. But the affair had a salutary effect on the Parliamentarians, warning them as Lancaster explained, 'not to be secure upon a victory, nor to neglect our guards.'[27] Two days later, the Royalists received encouragement of another kind when:

Some of Coll. Egerton's snapes up one of their sutlers who had bin bringing strong water to some of their guards, what money he received souldiers knew best, for they drank the King's health with it.[28]

5 November brought further distraction:

Wednesday is spent in prayer and thanksgiving. The night approaching our annual fires proclaim us protestants and hush their slanders into mere derision. Six of their guns are shot either to mock our joyes or else tell us that they had this day found a precident for Treason, worth their imitation.[29]

Parliamentarian snipers, particularly those occupying the steeple of St John's Church, continued to take their toll. On 7 November Lieutenant Morgell was killed whilst on guard near the Newgate, and next day, the sheriff, Ralph Richardson, was shot while at 'the bottom of Chickley the weaver's orchard… And buried next day with much lamentation.'[30]

A rumour was spreading among the citizens that the besiegers had begun mining operations aimed at creating new breaches in the walls. There is no evidence that this dangerous undertaking was actually begun, nor did Byron consider the threat to be serious, but he was concerned about its effects on morale:

> there was a strong report of the Enemy's mining, which terrified the people exceedingly; for prevention whereof I caused countermines to be made in all places where the wall was minable, which were not many, by reason for the most part it stood upon a hard rock.[31]

These activities seem to have been carried out near the Cathedral and around the breach at the Newgate.

Brereton was also facing problems. On 6 November there was a mutiny among Trained Band troops in the leaguer. They demonstrated outside the general's headquarters, 'using many unbecoming speeches' and demanding some of their five months' arrears in pay. There was a serious danger that, unless their demands were met, they would disband.[32]

On 8 November Brereton wrote to the Committee of Both Kingdoms, giving a mixed picture of his fortunes:

> We are still endeavouring to draw a line from water to water on the Welsh side, wherein were it not that we have received some interruption by a royal mount of the enemie's, lately made before we took the suburbs, and also by the extreme foul weather – which is so violent that our men cannot endure out of doors – it might have been in much more forwardnesse than it nowe is. Howsoever noe diligence nor endeavours shall be omitted that may conduce to the advance of this service, as touching which, I know not what more to add. Since we cast upp one mount att our bridge to secure it and another mount higher to confront their royall mount they can receive noe relief at all, seeing our men are quartered at Pulford, Bretton, Doddleston, Eccleston and Brewer's Hall, which doth so block up that side, that noe relief is brought or attempted to bee brought into the citty, which on the Chesire side is sufficiently begirt, for wee keepe our guards close to theire walls, and have cast upp and made such defences and breste workes against their gates, and sally-ports, as that there is noe great danger of theire issuing out to annoy and offend us in our quarters.[33]

Lord Byron, as Brereton admitted, had had considerable success in disrupting the besiegers' attempts to extend their siegeworks on the Welsh side of Chester. Thanks largely to Handbridge Fort, the Parliamentarian entrench-

61. Soldiers on campaign. The impact of campaign life, especially in winter, can be seen clearly in this contemporary view of men of the Spanish Army of Flanders. Though the besiegers of Chester were not threatened by actual starvation, troops on both sides suffered severely from the harsh weather.

ments never seem to have run further west than Eccleston Lane, allowing the Royalists to continue to infiltrate some supplies into Chester.[34]

For his part, Brereton was having continuing supply problems. Cheshire was becoming exhausted, and supplies were slow in arriving from elsewhere, especially from Wales, where:

> the people remaine soe disaffected that they rather prefer to bury and destroy or carry away than that our men should partake thereof or our leaguer have any benefit thereby.[35]

But Brereton was about to bring a powerful new weapon into play. On 7 November the Shropshire Parliamentarian committee informed Sir William that they were sending him their mortar, with a small amount of ammunition.[36] It would quickly make its presence felt.

9

'FIRE, FAMINE AND SWORD': NOVEMBER–DECEMBER 1645

Mortars played an important role in seventeenth-century siege warfare, especially in the destruction of property and in their effect on morale. They fired a projectile at a high trajectory but a low velocity. Frequently, as was probably the case at Chester, they were cast from bronze (often described by contemporaries as 'brass'). The shells they fired, usually termed 'granadoes', were of various kinds. One type was a hollow sphere filled with gunpowder, which exploded, ideally just above the ground, with shrapnel-like effects. Larger granadoes could be over 150lb in weight, and were both dangerous to handle and unpredictable in their effects. The timing of their explosion was, in theory, controlled by the length of the fuse fitted in a wooden socket in the projectile. But getting this right for a specific situation could cause problems. If the fuse was too short, the shell might explode prematurely, perhaps with fatal results for the mortar crew. If it were too long, the granadoe might bury itself harmlessly in the ground on impact, or be extinguished by the enemy. When practising, or for ranging purposes, either a shell case filled to the correct weight with earth or a large stone might be fired first. The latter were also sometimes used if ammunition was exhausted. Mortars were usually sited in specially constructed pits, with an observer reporting the fall of shot.

The targets of mortar fire were frequently out of direct sight, so exact accuracy was in any case not essential. This was particularly true of the type of projectile which seems to been mainly used at Chester. This was the incendiary, the simplest form of which consisted of a mixture of sulphur and saltpetre inside a canvas cover, or a ball of pitch and resin.

The main drawback of using mortars, at Chester as elsewhere, was the expense of the granadoes, which were irregularly supplied, usually in batches of twenty.[1]

John Tilt of Bromsgrove in Worcestershire was a noted mortar manufacturer, and it is very likely that the piece employed at Chester was manufactured by him. Brereton's mortar apparently first went into action on 10 November. Randle Holme describes its impact in characteristically florid terms:

> by this time they have unmusled death and swear theyle let him loose amongst us, a wide mouth'd mortar piece in which like the mouth of Etna spits little mountains in our faces, and grinds our dwellings into dust and ashes, three of these bombards or huge stones light amongst us, [possibly ranging shots] and the day following three more, the uncapt houses crouch from feare, and beg forbearance on their bended knees, but it seems these but forerun a greater judgement. Two great granadoes are by this time mounted, one of which being filled too full of spirit becomes its own executioner, by bursting in the aire, the other lights in a backside without doing any harm at all...[2]

The mortar bombardment, which initially was apparently more dramatic than effective, continued sporadically over several days. Holme describes some of the countermeasures taken by the defenders:

> But all this while our women like so many she astronomers have so glued their eyes to heaven in the expectation of a second thunder that they cannot easily be got to bed lest they dream of a granado, and indeed, not without cause, for the very next night [12 November] they toss us three granadoes and one huge stone, but they do no harm at all to maintaine that miracles have a being.
>
> They are quiet now until Sunday [15 November] and then they at night shoot six of their cannons, three at the Bridge, and three at the Eastgate, to put us in minde that they want nothing to complete their devilish undertakings in spite of opposition.[3]

Byron describes the effects of the mortar fire more prosaically:

> Immediately [Brereton] began to employ his mortars, first with stones to try their shooting, and then with granadoes of a great bigness, some of them being above six score pound weight, and some less. These

62. Mortar. 'Roaring Meg' is possibly the only surviving mortar of the Civil War period, and is similar to, and may actually be one of, those employed by the Parliamentarians at Chester.

granadoes were very terrible to the people, causing great spoil in the part of the Town where they fell. So that those who did not move further from the danger were forced to lodge in their cellars to avoid it. Yet the most affected part of them pleased themselves much with the observation that few of the granadoes fell, or at least did any remarkable harm, but in such houses, whose owners were suspected to be Roundheads, amongst whom, one, who had been a very forward man for Sir William Brereton in settling the militia in Chester, when the mortar pieces first began to play was much displeased at them, saying by that means Sir William might endanger his friends as well as his foes. And within a few nights after, a Granadoe fell into his house, which blew up, both him and it together. I gave orders that every householder should have a tub of water in readiness at his door, and that provision of raw hides should be made (as the best remedy against any fire that should be occasioned by the granadoes) the City for the most part consisting of old wooden buildings.

I likewise appointed sentinels to observe where the Granadoes fell, and immediately to give notice of them; and when the mortar pieces began to play (which commonly was about nine or ten o'clock at night and so continued till daylight) I caused the line to be manned, and the reserves to be in readiness, and walked the round myself, commanding

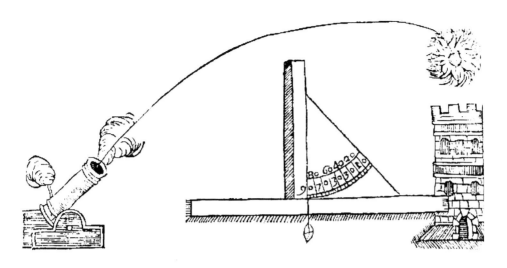

63. Mortar fire. The target of a mortar shell could be roughly calculated by means of the angle of elevation of the mortar, its distance, and observation of the fall of shot. However accuracy was generally low.

that no man should stir from his post, though the Town were all in fire, lest upon the concourse of people (which usually happens upon such occasions) either some treachery might be contrived within the Town, or some attempt by the Enemy without, to scale the walls in case they should find them neglected...[4]

Surviving records do not identify the unfortunate Parliamentarian supporter of Byron's anecdote, but in general the main areas of destruction, both in November and later, were along Watergate and Eastgate Streets.

No sooner had the bombardment begun than the defenders of Chester suffered another damaging blow with news of the surrender of Beeston Castle. The fortress's impregnable position had ruled out a Parliamentarian assault, but blockade had done its work as effectively, if more slowly, and by the middle of November the starving garrison could hold out no longer (they had, said Lancaster, been 'brought so low that they had eaten their catts, and had noe provision for that night.'[5]

The garrison received lenient terms, for Brereton had received reports of planned relief attempt from Holt, and a number of soldiers in his blockading force had deserted. Sir William reported the surrender to the speaker of the House of Commons:

I cannot but apprehend it my duty to let you know the goodness of God in restoring to us the strong Castle of Beeston today... We found in the Castle about eighty arms, some little ammunition, but less provision. The Governor, Captain Vallet, with about fifty of his soldiers, was permitted to march away on foot, with their arms, to Flint, and so to Denbigh and Beaumaris, there remaining about forty, who laid down their arms, and submitted themselves desiring liberty to live at home. The prize therein being found of very small value (but so much as it was) it is with equality to be distributed amongst the soldiers who have performed a very tedious siege... We found their horses in a weak and languishing condition (the Governor's own horse being scarce fit to go out the Castle).[6]

The fall of Beeston seemed to Brereton an opportune moment to test the resolution of Chester's defenders, particularly its citizens. So, on 18 November, a new summons, carefully worded to appeal to the civilians and divide them from Byron and the military, was issued.

When I call to mind those ancient and honourable privileges and immunities which the citizens and freemen of the city of Chester hath purchased by their former faithful service to the kingdom, I cannot but attempt all fair means on my part that may prevent the loss of these; the destruction of so famous a city, and the effusion of blood, which must needs ensue upon your continuance in that way you are against the Parl: and Kingdom...

But that it may appear to all that I desire to reduce, not ruin, that city, and that these may witness to those many inhabitants (now under your power) and to their posterity after them, that, if you hearken not thereunto, yourselves are the proper cause of the miseries of fire, famine and sword which must justly and unavoidably fall upon you, which I shall as much as possible endeavour to prevent...[7]

An unofficial truce followed for the remainder of the day, as Brereton reported that:

the soldiers did forbear shooting and did begin to discourse and debate familiarly and friendly, until such time as some of their officers came and did rebuke them upon the wall.[8]

64. Women 'fire-watching'. Although during periods of intense bombardment many civilians sought refuge in their cellars, the women of Chester played their part in watching for the fall of mortar shells and helping to fight the fires that they caused.

According to Sir William, Byron and the leading Royalists deliberately concealed the terms of his offer from the citizens, having frequently told them that the Parliamentarians would offer no quarter, and Lord Byron continued to spread reports of an imminent new relief attempt.

On 19 November he and Walley replied defiantly to Brereton's summons:

When we call to mind those ancient and honourable privileges and immunities granted theretofore to the citizens and freemen of the city of Chester for their loyalty to the crown, we cannot but wonder at your impertinence in urging that as an argument to withdraw us from our allegiance. Whereof (if all other respects were forgotten) we are obliged unto it even in point of gratitude as well as conscience. The care which you profess to preserve the city and to avoid the effusion of blood is so much contradicted by your actions that you must excuse us if we give credit rather to your deeds than words. As for the fire, sword and famine you threaten us withal upon the refusal of your unjust demands, we must tell you (blessed be God) we have less cause to fear them now than when you first sat down before this city, and doubt not of the continuance of his divine protection in the defence of this just cause wherein our liberties, religion and allegiance to our sovereign, whose service is inseparable from that of the kingdom, are so deeply engaged.[9]

Brereton responded angrily that:

it matters not what those people who are given over to destruction make lies their refuge write or pretend. By the tender of honourable conditions I have discharged my duty and conscience. Your blood is upon your own head and not upon your servant...[10]

Still in an irritated mood, Sir William told the Speaker:

you may guess that they either expect relief or suspect our weakness, unless stupid ignorance or stubborn infidelity possess them... Our siege is close, our soldiers resolved, our want is provision...[11]

Although less frequently than in the earlier stages of the siege, the Royalists continued to make sorties when occasion offered, and on 25 November Byron launched a major operation, admitted by Brereton to be 'the most adventurous and gallant they ever made.'[12] For over a month the Royalists had been increasingly hindered by the Parliamentarian bridge of boats which enabled the enemy easily to switch troops from one bank of the Dee to the other, and they planned a full-scale operation to destroy it. Sir William Brereton gives his version of what happened:

Yesternight the enemy had a design to have burnt our bridge over Dee, at the same time to have fallen upon our guards both of horse and foot beyond the water, and we verilie believe, when we had been in that distraction to have sallied out upon all our quarters... They about twelve o clock in the night issued out on the other side [out of Handbridge Fort] with a party of about eighty horse or more, and a considerable party of foot, forced in our sentinels to the high mount, which our men maintained gallantly, and our horse guard kept their ground, our foot gave them good store of shot, and after some of the enemy were fallen and others shot, they caused them to retreat before their relief came up to them, beat them to their mount. All this being in doing, at the same time two boats came up the river with the tide, filled with gorse, tallow, pitch, powder, and other combustable matter, and underneath them, and upon the sides of the boat in a frame of wood about twenty pieces of carbine barrels scarce full length and others pocket pistol length charged with powder and carbine bullets. The one of these came within six yards of the bridge and there fired, which gave a report like a peal of muskets, so that upon the higher ground all did verily believe they had been a company of musketeers. A soldier stept in, cast off the gorse and took the frame and brought it up with some six or seven of the pieces now discharged. The other boat gave fire over against my Lord of Derby's alley and fired all the gorse and the boat itself. We have found one of their men slain within forty yards of our mount, and believe more are slain and wounded. We have found four or five of their hand granadoes.[13]

According to Randle Holme:

Two boates well furnish't with all necessary combustibles await the coming of our engineer, whilst Lord St Pol, Colonel Egerton, Captain Crosby and Captain Dutton with all their troopes together with 100 foot are appointed to encounter such opposition as the enemy might possibly make to hinder our designe; the forlorne hope of horse is commanded by Captain Dutton and that of foot by Captain Bennet and by this time of being a very great spring tide and the flood advancing, our boates set forward, having within them divers chambers charged with small shot to annoy the enemy, if in case they should approach; but the tyde being somewhat slower than we expected, and too far spent for our purpose, the boates tire by the way, and come short of execution, firing them-selves (as it were for anger) that too tame a flood denyed their purpose, and cast their resolutions. Yet notwithstanding our horse and foot advance and skirmish with the enemy till they force them into a work of theirs made in the fashion of a halfe moone, which both secured their Bridge and warranted relief from the danger of our shot, our comman-ders perceiving this, retreat with the loss of two men slaine and about six shott, of which some after died.[14]

Byron's great effort had failed, and for the besieged Royalists as hope of relief and their remaining supplies dwindled together, the outlook was increasingly bleak. Even before the failure of the sortie, conditions in the city had been worsening. On 19 November Byron had ordered all the more sickly horses in the city to be turned out on the Roodeye to fend for themselves.[15]

Now re-supplied with ammunition, the Parliamentarian mortar resumed its bombardment. On 27 November, they sent us two Welsh granadoes [presumably the garrison believed, probably wrongly, that they had been fired from the Welsh side of the Dee] and beate down the end of a house in Eastgate Stree without doing any further harme. Next day they shott a woman that she died.[16]

Writing to the speaker on 28 November, Brereton voiced his frustration at Chester's continued defiance:

The besieged… remain still very obstinate, and do not seem inclinable to embrace any overtures made for their preservation… We cannot imagine upon what confidence they are induced to presume in this stubbornness, unless it be so that Sir Francis Gamull and Sir Richard Grosvenor… do enslave and inawe them hereunto, for if it be true what I have heard, Sir Francis hath wounded one or two with his own hand that were suspected to desire the delivery up of the city out of which we have heard very little…[17]

Although few Royalist forces were actually available, Brereton still feared another relief attempt. Rumour and incomplete reports greatly exaggerated the danger, and the besiegers received numerous false alarms concerning enemy movements. The defenders of Chester, though less active than before,

65. Bridge of boats site. The site of the Parliamentarian bridge of boats, looking across from its end on the Welsh side of the Dee to its terminus on the opposite bank.

66. Attempt to burn the bridge of boats. Fireboats, filled with explosive, had sometimes been used with devastating effect in similar situations on the Continent. At Chester, however, their launch seems to have been mistimed, rendering them ineffective.

also continued to make the occasional sally with small parties of horse to attack Parliamentarian outposts, and Brereton could only comfort himself with reports that:

> The better sort eat beef and bacon, but little cheese… the poorer sort of the city that are not soldiers are ready to starve, they are compelled to eat horseflesh.[18]

Almost daily skirmishes continued around the walls of Chester. On one occasion, a Royalist messenger carrying letters in cipher out of Chester was captured, but jumped off the bridge of boats and was drowned while attempting to escape. On 9 December, in a successful minor sally, the garrison destroyed a brick-built house near the eastern walls of the city, which had been providing the enemy with cover.[19]

A spasmodic mortar bombardment was continuing, and on 10 December the Parliamentarian piece, sited in the Foregate Street area, had its greatest success so far, as Randle Holmes describes.

> eleven huge granadoes like so many tumbling demi-phaetons threaten to set the city, if not the world, on fire. This was a terrible night indeed,

our houses like so many splitt vessels crash their supporters and burst themselves in sunder through the very violence of these descending fire-brands. The Talbott, an house adjoining to the Eastgate flames outright; our hands are busied in quenching this whilst the law of nature bids us leave and seek our own security. Being thus distracted another Thunder-cracke invites our eyes to the most miserable spectacle that spite could possibly present us with – two houses in the Watergate slippes joynt from joynt and creates an earthquake, the main posts josell each other, whilst the frighted casements fly for feare, in a word the whole fabrick is a perfect chaos lively set forth in this metamorphosis. The grandmother, mother and three children are struck stark dead and buried in the ruins of this humble edifice, a sepulchre well worth the enemye's remembrance…

But for all this they are not satisfied, women and children have not blood enough to quench their fury, and therefore about midnight they shoot seven more in hope of greater execution, one of these last light in an old man's bedchamber, and send him some fewe dayes sooner to his grave than perhaps was given him.

11 December six more break in amongst us, one of which persuade an old woman to bear the old man company to heaven, because the times were evill. Our ladyes all this while, like wise merchants, keep their sellers and will not venture forth in these tymes of danger lest they should miscarry, and indeed not without cause, for within the space of five nights following they shot twenty nine great granadoes which break down diverese houses in the Eastgate and Watergate streets, but very few or none at all hurt.[20]

Brereton was encouraged by reports reaching him of increasing food shortages in Chester. Some 'have lately fallen dead in ye streets for want, and others extremely pinched with hunger and all of them very miserable.'[21] Yet, on 13 December, he was forced to admit to the speaker that there was still no sign of a speedy end to the siege:

their extremities in the city are very great and their expectations are also very great that speedy relief will come to them, whereby they are encouraged in their obstinacy. We have made use of some mortar pieces, which we borrowed from Shrewsbury, whereby great execution hath been done. On 10 December fired in the night three several places in the city and killed and wounded several in their beds. Yet this doth nothing at all work upon them but they seem still to remain as stubborn as formerly, so as we judge it more easy to fire and destroy them than to reduce that strong city.[22]

Brereton continued to be concerned by reports of an imminent Royalist relief attempt. In reality, however, both lack of troops and bitter winter weather hindered any attempt by Lord Astley, the veteran Royalist officer who now commanded on the Welsh border.

The onset in earnest of winter was also keenly felt by both besieged and besiegers at Chester. Byron remembered that many of his Welsh troops sleeping on straw in a large school house suffered severely, while the citizens' (themselves suffering especially from lack of fuel with coal supplies from Wales cut off) charity towards them 'grew as cold as the weather'.[23] Brereton's men discontented by continuing pay arrears, were almost as severely afflicted, whilst to add to Sir William's problems, on 18 December he learnt that there were no more supplies of mortar ammunition available at Shrewsbury. Until he could find means to manufacture his own, he was reduced to firing large stones.[24]

However, reports from the increasing trickle of deserters escaping from the city gave him more grounds for optimism. On 17 December, two of them, John Fletcher and Giles Hurst of Gamull's regiment, told their interrogators that:

> The poorer sort are in extreme want and of late some of the Welsh soldiers have perished for want of food. He [Fletcher] chose rather to cast himself into the hands of the gentlemen of the Leaguer than to perish in the city. The soldiers are much discontented and have twice mutinied of late. Yet the Lord Byron and the great men in the city keep them together by informing them that relief is coming. He thinks they cannot hold out above a fortnight.[25]

Hurst added that most of the inhabitants were now subsisting on one meal a day, whilst:

> the soldiers, Irish and Welsh have 3d a day which they bestow in bread and beere to boil it in and that is their diet… The mortar peeces have done much execution in breaking and wrecking houses and slaying some persons, and the same are the greatest terror to them, nightly, at two of the clocke, and when the first goes off the women and children in general betake themselves to the cellars, the men to the walls.[26]

Within Chester Randle Holme wrote scathingly of the deserters 'a good riddance, it's better such rotten members were out, than in amongst us; far better to have an open foe than a treacherous friend.'[27] On 18 December a final weekly assessment of £200 was authorised for the maintainance of Wynne and Mostyn's regiments. The Welsh soldiers were to be 'hereafter duly paid, as they appear at the Parade, the sick and wounded only excepted.'[28]

By now the Dee around Holt was completely frozen over, causing Brereton concern that floating ice, or a sudden thaw, might wreck his bridge of boats. He was now being given detailed reports from within Chester by a prisoner, Lieutenant Philomen Mainwaring, who had been captured in October, and who, his exchange deliberately delayed, was now smuggling out reports of conditions within the city. On 21 December he reported:

> the town is in great distress and the poor cry out daily in the streets for want of meat, desiring the Mayor and Lord Byron to turn them out of town. Thereupon Lord St Pol (on Saturday last) hearing them cry out so, found fault with them; their reply to him was; 'Thou French rogue, hold thy tongue. We must obey thy commands and be starved to death.[29]

Though the Royalists still made occasional raids on enemy outposts, they now met with littler success, whilst the Parliamentarians replied with a desultory cannonade, which did little harm.

On 23 December another deserter, George Bavand, a twenty-year-old musketeer of Gamull's regiment, jumped down from the low section of wall near the Phoenix Tower and provided further evidence of the plight of Chester's defenders. There were, he said, twenty cattle left in the city, little or no corn, and no malt for brewing. The better-off could still eat well at a price – a turkey had been bought for Lord Cholmondeley, an elderly peer, at a cost of 17 shillings – but the level of discontent among the citizens as a whole was rising. The women 'gather themselves together every day crying out for relief to the governor and the rest of the commanders.'[30]

Christmas in Chester that year must have been a grim festival. The normally loquacious Randle Holme marked Christmas Day with the final brief entry in his journal:

> Because it is a festival, instead of stone they send us a token four granadoes, one of which burst among themselves.[31]

On 28 December Brereton's fears were realised when floating ice sank one of the boats supporting his bridge. The damage was not serious, and he hoped to have the bridge back in operation in about two days, but in the meantime his blockade on the Welsh side of Chester was stretched very thin. It provided the Royalist defenders of Chester with a final glimmer of hope in an increasingly desperate situation, for as Byron described:

> Provision now began to grow very short, both of corn and cattle, the greater part of which were killed up, except for some few milch kine, whose milk afforded more sustenance than their flesh could do; and horse flesh grew into such request that they who had any horses were forced to keep good guard upon them. The Welshmen could hardly keep themselves alive upon their threepence a day, and a third part at least of the City Regiment consisted of such, as with their families, had fled out of the Suburbs when the Enemy surprised them, and were forced to live upon the charity of others, which then began to be as cold as the weather. It fell out seasonably about the same time, that a hundred horse which I had been forced formerly to send out of town, for want of provisions, returned out of Wales one night with every one a bag of meal behind him, and back again safely by morning, which, though it were no considerable relief to so many mouths as were to feed in that City, yet much encouraged the people, to see that there was a possibility of relieving them, and extremely troubled the enemy, who thought the relief had been far greater than it was…[32]

The relief force was led by Major Cornelius De Wit, probably a Dutch professional soldier, of Robert Werden's regiment. As well as a small quantity of food, the relief force brought some money for the payment of the Welsh soldiers, probably obtained from their friends and relatives.

But on the same day, Michael Jones with a considerable force of horse took up position near Hawarden Castle, making any further such relief expedition virtually impossible. The situation of Royalist Chester was fast becoming hopeless.

10

SURRENDER: JANUARY–FEBRUARY 1646

By early January Lord St Pol, with a small party of horse including ten of his fellow reformadoes, had slipped out of Chester into North Wales to take charge of relief attempts. Archbishop Williams writing on 2 January to the Earl of Ormonde in Dublin, was not entirely pessimistic:

> Chester, with the help of some relief put in, on the Welsh side, may hold out three weeks, and much more, were not the poor unruly, who since the pulling down of so many suburbs, do pester that city. The Mayor's wife, always suspected, is gone to the enemie...[1]

Williams hoped that troops from Ireland, whom he urged Ormonde to transport with haste to North Wales, might still be able to co-operate with Astley in relieving Chester.

After his previous rebuff, Brereton was determined not to negotiate again until Chester's defenders asked for a parley. However he felt that some more or less gentle persuasion might not be out of place, and on 3 January drafted a letter, carefully aimed at the sensibilities of the citizens, of which copies were slipped into the town by the increasingly active Parliamentarian sympathisers there.

> You cannot but by this time be satisfied that those who have been averse to yielding up the city upon honourable terms have been your greatest enemie. Every day's continuance in your obstinacy begats increase of

your misery and charge and raises the resolutions both of officers and soldiers to exact the harder from you. Fall upon some speedy course to work your own peace before it be too late by delivering them up to the justice of the Parliament that are the most guilty, or enforcing them to deliver up the City. And you shall find that I will by all means endeavour to preserve and protect it from the ruin and devastation which will otherwise be speedily unavoidable.[2]

Significantly, there is persuasive evidence, in the shape of a post-war testimonial from Michael Jones, to suggest that Chester's mayor, Charles Walley, probably via his wife, was now in secret communication with Brereton regarding possible surrender conditions. This was not necessarily the action of one seeking only his own preservation. Walley, though a Royalist, was not an 'ultra' like Gamull and Grosvenor, and had been elected by the citizens to preserve as far as possible their own and the city's interests. He probably felt that his current actions were in furtherance of this obligation.

Brereton received further encouragement from another communication, on 4 January, from Lieutenant Philomen Mainwaring:

the town is in as ill a condition as almost you would wish; by reason the soldiers begin to mutiny every day. Upon Thursday last in the evening at the parade 300 Welshmen laid down their arms and told Lord Byron unless he would offer them more meat, they would do no more duty. Byron's reply was (openly) that if they would but hold the town 14 days, if there came no relief, he would surrender it. But that would not stop the simple Welshmens' mouths, for they cried out the more, in so much that Byron was enforced to forfeit the parade and leave them to their Welsh officers' persuasions, who could work no effect in them till such time as Byron sent money to appease their fury… In a word they be all hopeless of relief, both officers and soldiers, and I am of the opinion (and was likewise informed) that they desire you would summon the town, but their proud hearts will not suffer them to call a parley first…[3]

Brereton remained doubtful whether the time was yet ripe, but on 6 January was outvoted by his council of war, which resolved to send, next day, another summons to Chester.

Experience tells you on what foundation your hopes of relief were grounded: but that you may see my tender care of the preservation of the city and the lives and estates of the inhabitants, once more I summon you to deliver the city, castle and fort into my hands, for the use of King and Parliament.[4]

Brereton's trumpeter met with a frosty reception. He was refused admission to the town, and though some of the citizens appeared friendly, his summons was rejected by an officer, whose men then opened fire. Byron's uncompromising reply, written in his own hand but unsigned, was flung over the walls.

Keep your foolishly senseless paper to yourselves and know there are none in this city such knaves or fooles to be deluded thereby.[5]

Afterwards he explained his thinking. Still hoping that Astley, hovering around Lichfield, might mount a relief attempt, or that negotiations between the King and the Irish Confederates might bring military assistance, Byron:

forbore to give any answer (though much pressed thereunto by the Mayor and citizens… I thought it my duty to hold out the Town, as long as I could, though at the last I was sure to have the worse conditions, knowing that thereby I engaged an Army which (had it been at liberty) was designed to pursue the King wheresoever he went, and therefore I turned a deaf ear to all notions of treaty though then I might have had almost any conditions I could demand.[6]

Brereton was unsurprised at the reception his summons had received, 'as their wants in Chester are exceedingly great, so is their obstinacy and stub-bornness unparalleled.'[7]

67. Coins. As in other royalist garrisons, a mint was set up in Chester, probably in the castle, to produce coinage using such available material as the civic plate. This half-crown is believed to be a product of the Chester mint.

A trickle of supplies was still slipping through the blockade into Chester, carried by local men familiar with the paths through the marshes and byways and willing to take risks to gain the financial profits involved. An anonymous informant told the besiegers of the methods employed:

I am sorry to see so many as I do pass to Chester and back again, but I hope this… will make you more careful. There comes every day in the week four men and carry provisions in of the best, as pigs, turkeys, and other things for the great men, which makes them to stand out so. Sometimes there comes six or seven men and some of them carry pike staves on their shoulders. The way they go is through the Wayrookes [Wayrooks Bridge] and Poulton and along the water to Eaton. Sometimes they go through fields betwixt Poulton Green and Pulford and so to the Gorstella behind Dodleston… Their times of going from the Holt is two or three hours into the night and when they come back from Chester is about three or four o'clock in the morning.[8]

Though the few who could afford the prices asked might still obtain luxury goods by these means, the overall situation in Chester continued to deteriorate. Brereton's papers contain notes of the interrogation of James Sherrache, who had deserted the garrison the day Sir William sent in his latest summons:

was in the city when the summons was sent. Citizens exceeding troubled that the Lord Byron rejected it – a mutiny in the city this morning about provision. Cannot hold out a fortnight – so many will be starved. A Welsh captain was slain this night upon Castle from St John's steeple. Heard it was the Lord Byron ordered the Trumpet back. The letter which was thrown over walls – divers copies taken – and gents feare it will cause a mutiny among soldiers and citizens. Divers Welsh are dead from hunger. No drink to be bought nor any bread but what is got away by soldiers very early in the morning and all the day none to be bought. Five Welsh died last Saboth day, were starved, formerly there died twenty five in one week. No market these three weeks save for some oatmeal which was sold at 4d the quarter and a guard set to prevent the soldiers from taking it. Mortar did execution.[9]

Byron continued to play for time, and, despite increasingly impatient reminders, did not return a formal response to Brereton's summons until 12 January. He then, in a reply, which, as he expected, was rejected, offered to

68. Jacob, Lord Astley (1579–1652). A soldier of vast experience, Astley commanded the Oxford Army foot with reliability and competence for most of the war before being tasked in the winter of 1645/6 with raising a last Royalist field army along the Welsh border. He had some success in this, although he was never strong enough seriously to threaten the leaguer of Chester.

open negotiations if not assured of relief within twelve days. By now Lord Byron had obtained from the Royalist gentry and officers within Chester a signed undertaking 'to undergo the uttermost of extremities and to die with me in the defence of the City, rather than to be threatened into, or accept of, any treaty, to produce dishonourable terms.'[10] On 14 January Brereton angrily informed the Speaker:

> It seems many of the citizens remaine so enthralled and enawed as they dare not oppose nor resist; many more expect no less than inevitable ruin; were there no more guilt and charge upon them than to make reparation and satisfaction to those honest men whose estates they have seized and possessed after they had turned them out of Town. Hence it comes to pass that all former fair tenders have been rejected.[11]

Though faced with Chester's strong defences, and a continuing shortage of shells and powder for his mortar, Sir William expressed confidence in a speedy conclusion to the siege.

Indeed, within Chester's walls, Lord John Byron was beginning to despair:

All this while the wind stood fair out of Ireland, and daily expectation there was of the landing of those forces, though the prefixed time for their coming was elapsed, and no further news of them.[12]

With attempts to send in relief by water from Flint and Rhuddlan frustrated by the Parliamentarian ships, and by ice on the Dee, Byron, knowing that time was fast running out, ordered a full-scale search for food to be carried out in every house in Chester.

The survey was carefully organised. Officers and assembly members carrying out the search were instructed to arrest anyone unwilling to swear on oath to the truthfulness of their replies to the following questions:

1. What corn have you in your house, barn, or stable or in any other house, barn or stable or any place whatsoever? Declare the truth.
2. What in meat or bread, pease, beans, bran or fitches likewise in your own or any other house?
3. How many have you in family and what soldiers do you keep?
4. Do you know of anyone within this garrison that hath any store of corn threshed or unthreshed?[13]

Byron wrote that he had ordered the search because,

the want of all manner of provisions (especially of bread) grew extreme. So that some of the Welsh Soldiers died of famine, and most of them were grown so weak, that they were not able to pass upon duty, their lodging being as hard as their fare, and yet I took the strictest order I possibly could devise for the discovery of such provisions as might be concealed by particular persons, by appointing officers in every Ward of the city to search houses for victual and to examine the owners upon oath, what store of corn they had, allowing them a proportion for themselves and taking the surplus for the use of the garrison, at reasonable rates, and to prevent repining in others, began first at my own house, retaining a proportion of corn, and such other provisions as I had suitable to the number of my family and giving the rest to the public.[14]

The searchers were generally divided into pairs, a soldier and a civilian, one pair to each ward. While some evasion and concealment of supplies probably took place, their returns nevertheless provided grim reading, for it was obvious that provisions were almost exhausted.

Mr Richard Birde, 14 with souldiers, 6m[easures]. of corne, 2 m.
  of meale.
My lord Kilmory, 16 in fam. 4 soldiers, noe corne.
Mr Wm. Jones, 6 in fam., 5 soldiers, 40 coarse beans, scarce fit to
  be used.

In Eastgate ward, out of 160 families, 100 had no corn left.[15]

At around the same time, when murmurings in the town already almost
amounted to mutiny, the disaffected,

> insinuated to the People that notwithstanding their misery the Governor
> and Commissioners were well provided for. Lord Byron and some of the
> Commissioners took Opportunity severally to invite the Chief of the
> Malcontents to dine with them, and entertained them with boiled
> Wheat and gave 'em spring water to wash it down, solemnly assuring
> them that this and such like had been their Fare for some time past.[16]

It may be doubted how convincing such gestures were, and plainly imminent
starvation heightened the opposition to continued resistance. Byron noted:

> Both citizens and soldiers now began to be very impatient and mutinous,
> and multitudes of women (who are ever first employed in seditious
> actions upon the privilege of their sex) daily flocked about my house
> with great clamours asking whether I intended they should eat their
> children since they had nothing else left to sustain themselves withal.[17]

Byron blamed the mayor and assembly for failing to check these disorders,
claiming them to be enemy sympathizers who actually fomented the disorder,
alleging that:

> I valued a punctillo of honour more than all their lives and the safety of
> their city. I then found by sad experience what it was to be in a garrison
> consisting of Burghers whose obedience is tied more to their Mayor
> than their Governor.[18]

Some of Byron's accusations may have been exaggerated, but disaffection was
certainly rife, and the besiegers, kept informed of developments by their spies
and sympathizers within Chester, increased their pressure. Since the summons
of 7 January the Parliamentarian mortar:

had played much faster and did greater execution, having lately received a recruit of shells of greater size and much thicker than the former were. Every Granadoe that was shot now, caused a mutiny. And wheras before they used to curse Sir William Brereton for shooting them, they now railed at me [Byron] for giving him the occasion by holding out the Town.[19]

Propaganda sheets, which Brereton was firing over the walls or having handed to Royalist sentries at night were also having considerable effect.

Things being at this pass, and finding that if I consented not to a Treaty they would begin one without me, I called the Mayor, the Aldermen, and Council together, and told them I was as willing to treat as they were to have me, only desired them, not so to deface their former merit and services, as to do it in a mutinous and tumultuous manner, whereof the Enemy would take great advantage, and that to their prejudice, but if they would only leave it to me, I doubted not (how desperate soever they took their case to be) but to make honourable conditions for them…[20]

Byron added that he was confident that Astley was only awaiting reinforcements before marching to their relief, and that his approach might induce the Parliamentarians to offer better terms. The assemblymen correctly deduced this to be another attempt by Byron to spin out time, and,

With that I was interrupted by a confused clamour from them all, whereby I sufficiently understood their meaning, and at the same time there was a great concourse of people from all parts of the Town, to the Common Hall (where this meeting was) who all in a tumultuous manner, cried out for the Commissioners to be sent to Sir William Brereton to treat about the surrender of the Town. Whereupon (finding I could no longer delay it) I was advised by my friends (to avoid a greater mischief) to condescend to the opening of a Treaty.[21]

Byron, 'in regard of a resolution I had formerly taken, and declared upon the last uncivill reply of Sir William Brereton, to write to him no more', did not sign the letter which was sent to Sir William on 15 January, above the names of Charles Walley and Robert Tatton, acting sheriff, asking that negotiations might begin.[22] Brereton's reply was curt, for he was determined to take the hard line now that there was clear evidence of the defenders' failing morale.

69. Rioting. Although Chester would in any case have been forced to surrender within days, rioting and disorder among the civilian population, in which women played a leading role, undoubtedly hastened Royalist collapse.

> When I have so long considered of an answer to your letter as you, the Mayor, and Lord Byron took time to answer my summons you shall heare from me by a messenger of my own.[23]

Brereton's response in fact suited Byron very well. Indefatigable as ever,

> Now that I was forced to begin a Treaty, all my study was how to spin it out as long as might be, to the end that if my Lord Astley really intended my relief, I might keep myself unengaged, until he attempted it.[24]

Some reports suggested that there was still a chance of this happening. On 12 January Astley had written from Lichfield to Byron, saying that he would advance with 1,500 horse and 600 or 700 foot as soon as he had word that the promised Irish reinforcements had landed.

> I assure your Lordship I am very sensible how much the preservation of that place imports his Majestie's advantage, and I shall employ the utmost of my endeavours to render it relief, wherein I beseech your Lordship to be confident of…[25]

Other reports suggested that Astley would arrive by 24 January, while a correspondent assured Sir William Neale, governor of Hawarden Castle:

> Be pleased to know, that my Lord Astley, Sir Charles Lucas, Sir William Vaughan, and plenty of gallant Blades will be in these parts ere many days, with a sufficient force (by the blessing of God) to raise the siege.[26]

Both Byron and Sir William Brereton were now engaged in an elaborate game of bluff and counter-bluff, each seeking the best advantage when serious negotiations eventually opened, and Byron still desperately hoping that outside assistance would yet arrive in time. On 17 January, Sir William ostensibly 'allowed' two of his subordinates, James Lothian and Robert Duckenfield, to write to Walley and Tatton agreeing to consider Byron's proposals.

Lord Byron continued to stall for time, and an exchange of letters followed, Brereton becoming increasingly irritated by his opponent's delaying tactics. On 21 January, he angrily wrote to Byron:

> There is a vast difference betwixt the conditions you might have expected when first I summoned you, and those I can now afford you, yet that all the world may see that I desire not the increase of the Citty's miseries and charge I am contented (if you think your propositions of too high concernment to be sent by a trumpet) to grant a pass for any two gentlemen you will appoint to come along with them, and bring your propositions to my quarters this day or tomorrow by ten of the clock…[27]

Byron chose as his emissaries Sir Edmund Verney, one of his staff officers, and Thomas Thropp, a strongly Royalist member of the Brethren and major of Gamull's regiment. Once again his aim was to drag out discussions for as long as possible, for Astley had informed him of his intention to call a rendezvous at Bridgenorth on 27 January, prior to beginning his relief march on the next day. So Byron deliberately put forward propositions which he knew Brereton would find unacceptable, whilst urging Astley to make haste.

As expected, the Royalist proposals were rejected on 22 January. Nathaniel Lancaster described them as 'ridiculous, not fit to burden the Presse, or to reade, other than to make sport.'[28] Among Byron's demands were that he and his officers and men be allowed to march away with all their arms, horses, money and possessions, with a ten-day truce to follow in North Wales. No penalties were to be imposed on the citizens of Chester, or any oath of allegiance imposed on them, whilst the Parliamentarian garrison was to be composed entirely of Cheshiremen.

On Byron's instructions, his envoys refused to accept Bereton's counter proposals. Instead, Sir William had copies of them thrown over the city walls, and wrote angrily to Byron:

> I should not have expected propositions of so high demands as those you have sent. We know your wants are great, your hopes of relief desperate…[29]

Sir William was aware of the reasoning behind Byron's actions, and hurried on measures to tighten the screw on Chester still further, working on a new gun battery on the steeple of St John's Church, which would be able to command most of the city, and sending 1,000 horse under Colonel Thomas Mytton across the Dee towards Ruthin, to disperse the small force of horse and foot which Lord St Pol had mustered to support Astley. As a fighting force, St Pol's few hundred men, including the remnants of Lord Byron's own regiment of horse and about 160 mixed Irish and Lorraine mercenaries, were unimpressive, and melted away before Mytton's advance.[30]

Byron was not immediately aware of this latest and as it would prove, decisive, setback, but in any case his hand was now forced by the situation within Chester. 'In the meantime, the Treaty was forced on by a general mutiny of the soldiers, as well as inhabitants, notwithstanding my persuasion, and best endeavours to the contrary.'[31] Because of concerns for the safety of his family at the hands of groups of disorderly marauders who were increasingly roaming the streets, Byron had withdrawn to the castle, whose garrison, possibly consisting of his own Irish troops, was commanded by Lieutenant-Colonel Disney. From here on 27 January he wrote once more to Brereton:

> Sir,
>
> Those demands of mine, which you term unparalleled, have been heretofore granted by far greater commanders than yourself, no disparagement to you, to places in a far worse condition, than God be thanked, this is yet. Witness the Bosse, Breda and Maestricht, and as many other towns as have been beleaguered either by the Spaniards or the Hollanders; or to come near, York and Carlisle, or nearest of all, Beeston Castle; and therefore you must excuse me if, upon the authority of so many examples, I have not only propounded but think fit to insist upon them, as the sense of all manner of people in the city. As for your

conceit of demanding of myself, and the rest of the commanders and officers, to be your prisoners, I would have you know, that we esteem our honour so far above our lives, that no extremity whatsoever can put so mean thoughts into the meanest of us all. That to submit to your mercy is by us reckoned amongst those things that we intend never to make use of. I am nevertheless still content that the commissioners whose names I formerly tended unto you, meet with such as you shall appoint, in any indifferent place, to treat upon honourable conditions, and desire you to assure yourself that no other will be assented unto by,

your servant,
John Byron.[32]

Despite Byron's defiant words, Sir William was aware that Royalist Chester was at its last gasp, and his reply was both sardonic and uncompromising:

My Lord,

I cannot believe that you conceive the war betwixt the Hollanders and the Spaniards to be made a precident for us; neither can I believe that such conditions as you demand were granted to the Bosse, Breda or Maestricht. Sure I am, none such were given to York, Carlisle or Beeston, though some of them were maintained by as great commanders as yourself, and no disparagement to you. I shall therefore offer to your consideration the example of Liverpool, Basing and Lathom, who

70. Thomas Mytton (1597–1656) After commanding Parliamentarian forces in Shropshire, Mytton succeeded his brother-in-law, Sir Thomas Myddleton, as major-general in North Wales, and completed the reduction of the Royalist garrisons there.

by their refusal of honourable terms when they were propounded, were not long after subjected to captivity and the sword. You may, therefore, in pity to all those innocents under your command, tender their safety and the preservation of the city, for which end I have sent you fair and honourable conditions, such as are the sense of all the officers and soldiers with me, which being rejected, you may expect worse from your servant,

Wm. Brereton.[33]

Byron declined to reply personally, but on 28 January Walley and Tatton responded denying that Brereton's proposals had actually been rejected, and again requesting that their commissioners should meet to discuss terms.

Brereton agreed that talks should begin at 10 o'clock the next morning in Foregate Street, and sent Walley and Tatton a stern warning:

Gentlemen, Your several dilatory answers I have received and do assure you that if the Lord Byron, in whom (you say) the sole power to treat resteth, do not consent and act therein, you may forebear sending. Do not deceive yourselves in expectation that I will treat when you please. I am sorry my care for the city's preservation hath produced such unsuitable effects. The further misery that is like to befall the city on your own heads, and not on,

Your servant,
William Brereton.[34]

Byron had hoped to prolong talks for a further couple of days, having received another message from Astley, promising that he would rendezvous with St Pol at Llangollen on Saturday 31 January. However the Royalist commissioners returned from their first meeting on 29 January, not only with an account of what had been discussed, but with a report that Astley had retreated to Bridgnorth, news quickly confirmed by a despatch from Astley himself. These tidings caused a further mutiny, with Byron's authority in Chester rapidly collapsing.

So on 30 January Lord Byron again despatched his twelve commissioners, including representatives of his officers, the Royalist gentry and the assembly and clergy, this time with powers to conclude a treaty. Brereton in his turn had included a number of officers among his commissioners, because he wanted his soldiers 'to be better satisfied with what was agreed unto by their own officers', and the officers, he believed, would be more careful to keep the soldiers to an observance of those conditions, which they themselves had signed and ratified.[35]

The Royalist commissioners had hoped to delay proceedings for a another day or so, but in reality, now without hope of relief, they could only yield to the inevitable, and the treaty for the surrender of Chester, to take effect on the morning of 3 February, was agreed the same day.

The Articles of Surrender

I.   That the Lord Byron, and all Noblemen, Commanders, Officers, Gentlemen and Soldiers, and all other persons whatsoever, now residing in the city of Chester, and the castle and fort thereof, shall have liberty to march out of the said city, castle and fort, with all their apparel whatsoever, and no other or more goods, horses and arms, than are herafter mentioned, Viz: – the Lord Byron with his horse and arms, and ten men with their horses and arms, to attend him; also his lady and servants, two coaches, and four horses in each of them, for the accommodation of them and such other ladies and gentlewomen as the said Lord Byron shall think meet; with eighty of the said Lord's books, and all his deeds and evidences, manuscripts, and writings in his possession. And the said Lord and Lady, nor any of his attendants, shall carry amongst them all above forty pounds in money, and twenty pounds in plate. The rest of the Noblemen with their ladies and servants, to march with their horses, each of the said Lords, attended with four men, their horses and arms; and every such Nobleman carrying with him not above thirty pounds in money. Every Knight and Colonel to march with two men, their horses and arms; no such Knight or Colonel to carry with him above ten pounds in money. Every Lieutenant-Colonel, Major, and Captain of horse, with one man their horses and arms; and such Lieutenant-Colonel, Major, and Captain, not to carry with him above five pounds in money. Every Captain of foot, Esquire, Graduate, Preaching Minister, Gentleman of quality, the Advocate and Secretary of the army, every one of them with his own horse and sword, the Ministers without swords; none of them carrying with him above fifty shillings; and the Ministers to have all their own manuscripts, notes and evidences. Lieutenants, Cornets, Ensigns, and other inferior Officers, in commission, on foot, with every man his own sword, and not above twenty shillings in money. All troopers, soldiers, gun powdermakers, cannoniers, and all others, not beforementioned, to march without horse or arms; and that none of the said persons beforementioned shall, in their march, after they are out of the city and the liberties thereof, be plundered, searched, or molested.

II.   That all women, of what degree soever, that please to march out of the city, shall have all their apparel with them; and such officers wives whose husbands are absent, may carry such sums of money with them as are allowed by these articles to commanders, officers or gentlemen, of their husbands' qualities and no more.

III.   That none of the commanders, officers or soldiers, or any other, at or before their marching out of the city, castle, or fort, injure or plunder the person or goods of any; nor carry anything away out of the city, castle, or fort, but what is their own, and hereby allowed.

IV.   That all citizens and others now residing within the city, shall be saved and secured in their persons, and their goods and estates within the city and liberties thereof be preserved and kept from the plunder and violence of the soldiers; and have the like freedom of trade as other towns under the Parliament protection have, and such immunities as they of right ought to have. And that every merchant and tradesman of Chester as shall desire to go into North Wales to look after his goods, shall have a pass to go thither and return back again, he first giving security that during his absence he will do no act to the prejudice of the Parliament; and that no such person shall at any time without license, carry more with him than sufficient to defray the charges of his journey. And that all citizens, and other inhabitants, who shall now or hereafter desire to march out of the city of Chester, and not to act anything against the Parliament, their wives and families to have the benefits and privileges of inhabitants.

V.   That such officers or soldiers as shall be left sick or wounded within the city of Chester, or the castle, or the fort, thereof, shall have liberty to stay till their recovery, and have passes or convoy to any of the King's garrisons not blocked up, in the meantime to be provided for.

VI.   That the said Lord Byron, Noblemen, commanders, gentlemen, officers, and soldiers, and all others that shall march out of town, shall have liberty to march to Conway, and five days are allowed them to march thither, with a convoy of two hundred horse; the Welsh officers and soldiers shall have liberty to go to their own homes, all of them to have free quarters on their march, and twelve carriages if they shall have occasion to use so many, which carriages are to be returned on the sixth day, and that passes be given them for their safe return to Chester, and that they be secured until they return thither.

VII.   That no soldier on his march shall be inveigled or enticed from his colours or command, with any promise or inducement whatsoever.

VIII. That all such persons, citizens, or others, that have families in Chester, and are now in places remote, shall have the like benefit of these articles, as those who are now resident in the city.

IX.   That the friends of the Earl of Derby, and Lichfield, or any of those whose dead bodies are not yet interred in Chester, shall have two months time to fetch them thence, provided that none of them come attended with above twenty horses.

X.   That no church within the city, or evidence, or writings belonging to the same, shall be defaced.

XI.   That such Irish as were born of Irish parents, and have taken part with the rebels in Ireland, now in the city, shall be prisoners.

XII.   That all those horses and arms belonging to those that march out, and not by these articles allowed to be taken and carried out of the city, except such horses as are the proper goods of the citizens and inhabitants that shall remain in the city before the delivery of the same, be brought, the horses unto the castle court, and the arms in the shirehall, where officers shall be appointed to receive them.

XIII. That in consideration of this, the said city and castle without any slighting or defacing thereof, with all the ordnance, arms, ammunition, and all other furniture and provision of war therein whatsoever, except what is allowed to be carried away and herein mentioned, with the County Palatine Seal, Sword, and all the records in the Castle without diminuation, embezzling, or defacing be delivered to the said Sir William Brereton, or such as he shall appoint, for the use of King and Parliament upon Tuesday next, being the third of this instant February, 1645 [1646] by ten of the clock in the forenoon.

XIV.   That the fort, with all ordnance, arms, ammunition, and provisions therein, of what sort soever, not firmly granted or allowed of upon the signing of these articles be delivered to Sir William Brereton or such as he shall appoint.

XV.   That upon the signing of these articles, all prisoners in the city, castle or fort, that have been in arms for the Parliament, or imprisoned for adhering thereunto, shall be immediately at liberty.

XVI.   That the convoys shall not receive an injury on their journey, going or coming back, and shall have three days allowed for their return.

XVII.   That if any persons concerned in any of these articles, shall violate any part of them, such persons shall lose the benefit of the said articles.

XVIII. That upon signing of the articles, sufficient hostages (such as shall be approved of) be given for the performance of the said articles.[36]

Several of the more die-hard Chester Royalists among the commissioners, including Sir Francis Gamull, Thomas Cowper, and surprisingly, perhaps, Charles Walley, refused to sign the articles, but the terms were carried back to Lord Byron, who accepted them. With characteristic animosity, he later described them as:

> for myself and the Officers with me… as good as in such an exigient I could expect, and those for the citizens as ill as I could wish, their folly as well as knavery deserving no better.[37]

Byron was probably correct in the first part of his statement. With Royalist resistance in Chester likely to break down hourly, Brereton could probably have soon enforced a virtually unconditional capitulation. The citizens of Chester, however, apart from the huge material loss they had suffered, came out of the siege with the remains of their city unplundered, and with their privileges and trading rights intact. Whatever his personal animosity towards them, Brereton had no intention of destroying one of the major sources of local prosperity.

Sir William, like other Parliamentarian commanders, was theoretically bound by an Ordinance of Parliament decreeing death for any native Irishmen found serving in the Royalist forces. The hundred men of Byron's regiment of foot were certainly included in this category, and according to the terms of the surrender should have been handed over. Byron made particular efforts to exempt them from the penalty, and, although the Parliamentarian commissioners could not officially agree, they were quietly allowed to depart with the rest of the garrison, whilst Brereton told the speaker that he still had to verify the number of Irish in the town.

Colonels Hugh Wynne and Henry Waite were handed over as hostages for the Royalists' observance of the terms, whilst the Parliamentarian commanders Colonels Bowyer and Massey were held hostage at Holt Castle in return.

On the morning of 3 February 1646, Byron's men piled arms, some 2,000 of them, and 520 headpieces, in the castle courtyard, and then, with their commander at their head, marched out for the last time over the Dee Bridge bound for North Wales.

71. Surrender. On the morning of 3 February 1646 the Royalist garrison of Chester march out for the last time across the Dee Bridge, watched by the victors.

Unlike some other capitulations, when surrendered troops were plundered, the defeated Royalists at Chester were treated with respect. It is tempting to imagine some symbolic personal encounter between those two sharply differing protagonists, Lord John Byron and Sir William Brereton. But there is no evidence that the two men ever met face to face. Sir William may well have been watching with quiet satisfaction from the nearby high ground, as, leaving the western gatehouse of the Dee Bridge, Byron and his men were met by Major Jerome Zanckey and his escort of horse, on the first stage of their march to Conway.

The great siege was over, and Chester, battered, starving and impoverished, awaited with apprehension the judgement of its conquerors.

II

AFTERMATH

Though Chester had fallen, fighting continued in its neighbourhood for some time longer. Byron, by virtue of his commission as 'Field Marshal General of North Wales and those Parts', established himself at Caernarvon, where he endeavoured to keep resistance alive in the fading hope of reinforcements from Ireland. Parliamentarian forces had to reduce the numerous castles of the area in a series of siege operations. They came under the overall command of Colonel Thomas Mytton, and the first garrisons to surrender to him were two of Chester's nearer neighbours: Chirk fell on 28 February and Hawarden on 13 March. Ruthin Castle surrendered on 12 April, and then Mytton moved against Byron's headquarters at Caernarvon. Resistance here continued until 4 June, when the garrison surrendered on terms. Lord Byron and his officers, who included a number of stalwarts of the siege of Chester, including Colonels Vere and Vaine, Lieutenant-Colonels Disney and Robinson and the hero of Rowton Heath, Jeffrey Shakerley, were allowed either to make their peace with Parliament or to go abroad. Byron, a convinced Royalist, and also perhaps prevented from staying in England by his mountainous debts, headed for Ireland and France to continue serving the King.

At Conway, where Sir John Owen was in command, Archbishop Williams switched sides, and was with the Parliamentarians when the town was stormed on 8 August. A number of Irish, including some of Lieutenant-Colonel Little's men of Byron's regiment, were among the prisoners, and this time their luck ran out. Possibly because they were captured in the heat of battle, and because the hardline Mytton was angered by what he saw as increasingly futile Royalist resistance, they were 'tied back to back, and cast overboard and sent by water to their own country.' Others, who were in Conway Castle, were more fortunate. Owen only surrendered it on 18 November, and the surviving Irish seem to have been shipped home.

Rhuddlan Castle, whose governor, Sir Gilbert, was the last of the Byron brothers still in arms, fell at the end of July; and Flint, with Roger Mostyn amongst its defenders, in August. Denbigh held out until October, and Sir Richard Lloyd, who had been under blockade for over a year, did not yield Holt until 13 January 1647. Last of all, in March, was Harlech, with Sir Francis Gamull and Hugh Wynne among its garrison.[1]

Chester itself had not welcomed the new regime. In February 1646 Brereton wrote to the speaker:

> The city itself is generally disaffected towards us, so that without a strong force we shall be unable to secure the city, or ourselves no less than 1,500 foot and 200 horse being sufficient for that work. It will also require a large sum of money to lay in a magazine of ammunition, to have a store well furnished with provisions, and also to alter and strengthen the fortifications, which cannot be done without assistance from neighbouring parts.[2]

Chester's fear of Sir William's vengeance proved to be unfounded. Brereton and most of his army were speedily called away to undertake the siege of Lichfield, and to take part in the final operations which led to the surrender of Lord Astley and the last Royalist field army on 21 March at Stow-on-the-Wold.

The first Parliamentarian governor of Chester was the pragmatic professional soldier Colonel Michael Jones. The city which he took over was shattered, embittered and exhausted by its experience of war. Randle Holme compiled a catalogue of the destruction. All of the suburbs of Great Boughton and Chrisleton, all of Foregate Street, Cow Lane, and St John's Lane 'with those houses next the Eastgate' had been burnt and destroyed. The Northgate suburbs had been razed to the ground, and the unfortunate inhabitants of Handbridge had seen their homes burnt, then rebuilt, then burnt again. The glovers' houses under the walls of the city, and the fulling mills, had been destroyed, while the Parliamentarian bombardment had wreaked devastation within the walls of the old city itself.

> The destruction of divers other houses in the cittie, with grenades, not a house from Eastgate to the middle of Watergate Street on both sides but received some hurt by them, many slaine by the fall of houses which

were blowen up, St Peter's Church much defaced and pews torne, and all windows broken by two granadoes that fell therein.

In the adjacent countryside, at least six large houses – Blacon, Bache, Hoole, Bretton and Flookersbrook Halls – had been destroyed. The financial loss which Chester suffered from all causes is impossible to calculate accurately, but was estimated by Holme to be in the region of £200,000 – 'So farre hath the God of Heaven humbled this famous cittie.'[3]

Losses had been suffered by all classes. Thomas Thropp, as well as being briefly imprisoned on the fall of the city, had a number of properties destroyed, and faced the prospect of a hefty fine for his 'delinquency.' Charles Walley had had three houses burnt, including the house in Foregate Street which for a time had served as Brereton's headquarters, the 'Red Lyon' inn and a house and barn in Boughton. Gamull's Dee mills were confiscated. John Johnson, a Royalist alderman and shoemaker, later petitioned for assistance, saying:

> in time of the late siege, he had received great loss by fire, having had two houses and a kiln burnt to the ground, besides many household goods, and that he had all his boots, shoes, materials for his trade, and other things, burnt in his shoppe, and he had a wife and six small children to maintaine...[4]

The cost of the siege in human lives is impossible to quantify, but must have run into several hundreds of Chester's citizens, and before the city could begin to recover it suffered another severe blow with the return of plague. The weakened health of many of the inhabitants, resulting from the privations of the siege and the still overcrowded conditions in which they lived, meant that they fell easy victim to the epidemic. Between 22 June 1647 and 20 April 1648 over 2,000 people, probably at least 20% of the inhabitants, died very unpleasant deaths:

> The Plague takes them very strangely, strikes them black of one side, then they run mad, some drowne themselves, others would kill themselves, they dye within a few houres, some run up and downe the streetes in their shirts to the great horror of those in the Citty...[5]

Many must have fled to the surrounding countryside in an attempt to avoid infection, and so depopulated was Chester that grass was said to be growing in the streets around the High Cross in the centre of the town.

As well as the effects of war and pestilence, Chester and its economy also suffered after the siege from a period of administrative confusion. The merchant guilds temporarily lost their monopolies with the result that a number of 'strangers' took over businesses in the city.

The government of Chester took some time to sort out. Virtually all of the leading figures in the city, including Charles Walley, Nicholas Ince, Randle Holme, Thomas Cowper, Thomas Thropp, Francis Gamull, Robert Brerewood and a large number of others, were formally removed from office in October 1646. But finding replacements for them proved far from easy. The predominantly Royalist sentiment of Chester is demonstrated by the fact that after the Parliamentarian William Edwards had been appointed mayor, and various other citizens who had been expelled from Chester by the Royalists were given posts, it was still necessary to appoint at least six men who had served in the Royalist assembly, including John Johnson, who, along with Charles Walley, had represented the citizens' views in 1643 to the King. Even then the last vacancies were not filled until October 1648, and only after this was the assembly able to begin functioning normally again.

The threat of war returned briefly with the series of uprisings and the Scottish invasion of 1648, known as the Second Civil War. Royalist plotters, organised by Lord Byron, who had secretly returned to England, schemed to seize Chester Castle, but they were betrayed before their plans could be put into operation.

The revived assembly was a sign of Chester's gradual recovery. With remarkable speed, the city authorities again began to assert their independence from national government. The Dee mills, for example, had been handed over to William Edwards, after Parliament had passed an Ordnance ordering their demolition, but the assembly disputed both this and their possession by Edwards, and the demolition was not carried out.

During the 1650s rebuilding began in both the old city and the suburbs, and proceeded at a rapidly increasing rate. It is to this period that some of the best-known buildings in Chester belong, for example 'God's Providence House' in Watergate Street, built to replace a house destroyed during the siege.[6]

The final convulsion of Civil War took place in 1659, when Brereton's old rival Sir George Booth launched his pro-monarchy rising. The Chester assembly sympathised with Booth, and went so far as to raise two companies of troops in his support. But the rebels failed to secure Chester Castle, and the rising collapsed with Booth's defeat on 19 August at Winnington Bridge.

Chester had been fortunate that an ultimately doomed rebellion had ended so quickly without the city suffering further damage, while any penalties which the citizens might have suffered as a result of their ambivalent attitude were nullified by the restoration of King Charles II in May 1660.

The restoration made little material difference to a city which had already regained most of its privileges and independence, and which was a fair way towards recovering its former prosperity. But it must have been with the feeling of using a well-deserved title, that Chester's assembly, in its addresses to the King, henceforward gave their city the title of 'Ancient and Loyal'.

It remains to look at the fates of some of those personalities who had played a major role in the story of Civil War Chester.

Sir William Brereton laid down his military command at the end of the First Civil War, and returned as an MP to Westminster. But he was never again to achieve any particular prominence. He apparently sided with the army in its dispute with Parliament, but was an unenthusiastic participant in the process leading to the execution of King Charles I. Henceforward he concerned himself with local and family affairs, and by the restoration had sunk into a degree of obscurity which made the Royalists decide against bringing to him to account for his earlier activities. Brereton died in May 1661 at his home in Croydon; according to an unconfirmed tradition, his coffin was swept away in a swollen river while being taken back to Cheshire for burial.

Colonel Michael Jones, the self-confident professional soldier who had commanded the Cheshire horse with such efficiency, returned to the Parliamentarian forces in Ireland. He won the decisive battle of the Irish war at Rathmines on 2 August 1649, and died soon afterwards of fever.

In 1648 James Lothian, commander of Brereton's foot, serving as a colonel, helped Thomas Mytton suppress the Royalist rising in North Wales, and then disappeared from recorded history.

The colourful Colonel-General Sydenham Poyntz continued his eventful career. He remained commander of the army of the Northern Association until the summer of 1647, when, as a Presbyterian 'moderate', he lost his position when his men mutinied and replaced him with John Lambert. Poyntz fled first to the West Indies, where he was briefly Royalist governor of the Leeward Islands, and then to Virginia, where he was still alive in 1663.

Royalist fortunes were equally mixed. Lord John Byron, after the failure of his attempts in 1648 to kindle Royalist rebellion in his old command of North Wales and its borders, was declared by Parliament to be a perpetual traitor, proscribed and banished. He returned to Ireland, then went to France, where he was high in the counsels of the new King, Charles II, and was appointed comptroller of the Duke of York's household. Byron died in Paris in 1652, his death described as an 'irreparable loss' to the Royalist cause. His young wife, Lady Eleanor, found consolation as a mistress to King Charles II.

That other arch-Royalist, Sir Francis Gamull, left the country after the surrender of Harlech in 1647. He compounded with Parliament in 1649, but was involved in the rising of 1651, and died in obscure circumstances, either in that year or 1654.

Sir Edmund Verney returned to Ireland after the end of hostilities on the mainland, and was killed in the slaughter following Cromwell's capture of Drogheda in 1649.

Sir Marmaduke Langdale saw action again in 1648, as leader of the northern Royalists, made a hazardous escape to the Continent, fought there as a professional soldier, and died in semi-poverty soon after the restoration.

The 'Devil of Shrawardine', Sir William Vaughan, also returned to serve in Ireland, and, over sixty years of age, was killed in action against his old opponent, Michael Jones, at Rathmines.

Roger Mostyn, whose regiment of foot had been a mainstay of the defence of Chester, was a notable Royalist conspirator during the interregnum. He was created a baronet at the restoration, and held various public offices in North Wales until his death in about 1690.

Colonel Hugh Wynne, that other stalwart of Chester's resistance, was in Denbigh and Harlech garrisons, compounded in 1649, and then served with the Parliamentarian forces in Ireland. At the restoration he became a JP, a deputy lieutenant, and an officer of the Trained Band. He died in 1674.

Finally the enigmatic and unclassifiable Charles Walley continued his career as a great survivor. In his composition statement of 1649 he claimed that he had assisted the Parliamentarians in all ways possible after the fall of Chester, and was supported in this by Michael Jones, who added that Walley had been responsible for a constant stream of intelligence reports to the besiegers. In June 1649, the authorities discharged Walley from all imputations of delinquency and declared him capable of holding any office of trust under the Commonwealth! He resumed his place as an alderman, and in 1654 was chosen as Chester's MP in the in the Protectorate Parliament.

In some ways Walley typified Chester itself; resourceful, enduring, and, above all, determined to survive.

APPENDIX
A TOUR OF CIVIL WAR CHESTER

Among the historic riches of Chester, much that related to the Civil War has disappeared over the centuries. The extensive earthworks, for example, constructed by both sides during the siege were mostly demolished at the end of hostilities, and most surviving remnants disappeared during the expansion of the suburbs in succeeding years.

Within the old city itself, the destruction resulting from the siege led to the loss of many fine buildings, and most of those that survived were extensively altered in later years. Though many of the houses and shops in the centre of Chester retain evidence of origins prior to the Civil War, this is often not readily apparent, and most of the famed half-timber buildings are of later date.

However a good deal survives to be discovered by the visitor. It is suggested that a tour should begin with the most famous and visible feature, the city walls, a circuit of which should best be commenced by the Dee, at the Bridgegate.

Known originally as the Welsh Gate, the old gate, distinguished by John Tyrer's water tower which stood on its western side, was demolished in 1782, and replaced by the present gate. From its top the Dee Bridge is plainly visible, and, apart from slight widening, remains much as it was during the siege. The guard tower and drawbridge which stood at the Welsh end have long since disappeared. Across the river is the suburb of Handbridge. Little trace of the siege remains here; the exact site of Lord Byron's 'royal mount' is unknown, though it was probably situated on the rising ground above the Dee Bridge.

At the Chester end of the bridge is a disused hydro-electric station which stands on the site of some of the Dee mills which were a target of Parliamentarian artillery fire. Other mills were situated along the bank of the Dee now occupied by the riverside promenade known as the Groves. The last mills were demolished in 1910, but just upstream from the Dee Bridge may still be seen the remains of the weir associated with them.

Proceeding along the walls, just to the east of the Bridgegate are the remains of one of the defensive towers of the original gateway. Here, as elsewhere, the walls were greatly altered in the course of the extensive eighteenth-century reconstruction which turned them into a promenade for the citizens.

Moving on again eastwards, the next feature of interest (best inspected from the car park of the restaurant below) is Barnaby's Tower, which stands at the south-eastern angle of the walls. Looking up from below, it is possible to distinguish the marks made on the tower by cannon shot from the Parliamentarian batteries mounted near St John's Church.

Proceed northwards towards the Newgate, and, as you approach the stretch of wall overlooking the area known as the Roman Garden, look over to the east, across the Roman amphitheatre to St John's Church. The tower of the church, from which Parliamentarian snipers harassed the defenders of Chester, collapsed over a century ago, but the ground on either side of the church, on which Parliamentarian batteries were sited, may be seen either from the walls or by visiting the church itself, in order to gain a 'besiegers' eye view'.

Descending from the wall at the Newgate, enter the Roman Garden. Here, careful examination of the face of the wall shows the repair work carried out on the breach made by the Parliamentarians in September 1645. The present Newgate is a modern structure, erected last century, but the old gate, now called the Wolf Gate, still stands next to it.

Returning to the city walls, cross the remains of Thimbley's Tower, damaged during the siege, and approach the Eastgate. The modern gate bears little resemblance to the impressive structure of the Civil War period, which was demolished in 1764, but it provides an excellent vantage point to look eastwards along Foregate Street in the direction of the Bars. The present array of chain stores and modern commercial developments contain few reminders of the Civil War, which is hardly surprising given that most of the suburbs in this area were razed to the ground in the course of the siege. The view westwards along Eastgate Street towards the High Cross and Watergate Street gives some idea of the cramped conditions and relatively small area within which the defenders were confined during the later stages of the siege.

Continuing northwards, opposite the modern Bell Tower near the cathedral is Frodsham Street, known in the seventeenth century as Cow Lane, and also heavily damaged during the siege. Here, as elsewhere, the suburbs contain little to remind us of the Civil War.

Just to the north of the present Kaleyard steps was the Saddlers' Tower, of which no trace now remains. This stretch of wall, which was relatively low (though higher than now), witnessed some of the heaviest fighting of the siege.

On the north-east angle of the walls is the King Charles or Phoenix Tower, from which King Charles witnessed the closing stages of the battle of Rowton Heath, and which until recently housed a small Civil War museum.

The walls now turn westwards, and the following stretch is the most impressive of the whole circuit, with the Shropshire Union Canal occupying the site of the defensive ditch that was still in existence at this point during the Civil War.

The Northgate is another relatively modern structure, replacing the original gateway demolished in 1810, but the succeeding stretch of wall includes two interesting relics of the siege. Just to the east of the modern St Martin's Gate is the rectangular structure known, after a Royalist officer during the siege, as Morgan's Mount. In fact the actual Morgan's Mount of the siege was part of the outworks below the wall, and it was not until the nineteenth century that the name was applied to what was probably a gun platform during the siege.

Just to the west of here is Pemberton's Parlour, the greatly altered remains of the Goblin Tower, which was originally a circular structure spanning the width of the wall. Somewhere near here was the site of the second breach made by Parliamentarian artillery. The exact spot remains unidentified, and may have been in the section of wall demolished in the nineteenth century during the construction of the railway.

At the north-west angle of the walls are two more original towers, Bonewaldesthorne's Tower and the Water Tower. Neither is recorded as playing any notable role in the siege, but in the spur wall connecting them note the medieval embrasures which the Civil War garrison converted into gun ports.

The stretch of wall between the Water Tower and castle has largely been converted into a promenade, and, protected by the Dee, was never as formidable as the remainder of the circuit. To the right, towards the Dee and Wales, is Chester Racecourse, occupying the enlarged site of the Roodeye, and on which the stump of the cross that gave it its name may still be seen. On the rising ground beyond the river was the site of the Parliamentarian Brewer's Hall battery.

At the south-west angle of the defences is Chester Castle. Following extensive reconstruction in the nineteenth century, this has little resemblance to the building of the Civil War period, though some medieval work remains, notably Agricola's Tower. Passing on, we reach Bridgegate, completing the circuit.

Within the walls are a number of sites and buildings associated with the Civil War period. St Werburgh's Cathedral was heavily restored during the nineteenth century, and although a number of Civil War notables, such as Colonel John Marrow, were buried within its confines, little remains directly to remind us of the siege. The nearby Cathedral Close contains several houses built in the early part of the seventeenth century.

In the town centre, where Bridge Street, Eastgate Street and Watergate Street meet, are the remains of the High Cross. This was formerly a two-tiered, six-sided structure with religious figures mounted in its niches. It was demolished by the Parliamentarians after the capture of Chester, but some fragments, buried beneath the steps leading to adjacent St Peter's Church, were later discovered, and eventually, in 1975, erected in their present position.

Along the south side of St Peter's Church was the Pentice, a two-storey building, with shops on its lower floor and municipal offices above them. The latter were used as a guard room and armoury during the siege. The Pentice was demolished at the end of the eighteenth century, though some traces of it can still be seen on the stonework of the church wall.

Eastgate Street retains few buildings obviously dating from the time of the siege, though the Boot Inn is said to have been commenced in 1643, whilst No. 32 (Mappin and Webb's) contains some Jacobean timber work. Northgate Street contains the Blue Bell Inn, a largely fifteenth-century building.

Watergate Street, however, is rich in contemporary buildings. The Stanley Palace of the 1590s is close by, together with the Guildhall, formerly Holy Trinity Church. Other noteworthy houses include Bishop Lloyd's House on the south side of the street, Leche House, and 'God's Providence House' (the latter most likely an example of the widespread rebuilding of the 1650s). Many other buildings include seventeenth-century features.

In Bridge Street note No. 12 (now Bookland), which was the residence of the Royalist Cowper family.

Lower Bridge Street also contains some notable buildings. On the eastern side , at the junction with Pepper Street, St Olave's Church now houses the Chester Heritage Centre, with an interesting Civil War exhibition. On the western side of the street the Tudor House was built in 1603, whilst on the same side of the street is the heavily restored Gamull House (now a restaurant), the residence of Sir Francis, and where the King lodged in 1645. The 'Old King's Head' inn was originally built by Randle Holme; while on the corner of Lower Bridge Street and Grosvenor Street the 'Falcon' was the town house of the Grosvenor family, and was extended by Lieutenant-Colonel Sir Richard Grosvenor in 1643.

Of the network of less permanent fortifications and siegeworks little remains. It is said that Rock Lane, north of the city walls, is the site of the 'great trench' dug by Prince Rupert in 1644. Of all of Brereton's siegeworks, the only surviving trace lies just across the river from Dee Lane, site of the Parliamentarian bridge of boats. Here, on the Queen's Meadows, some irregularities of ground mark the position of the 'mount' which guarded the Welsh end of the bridge.[1]

MAPS

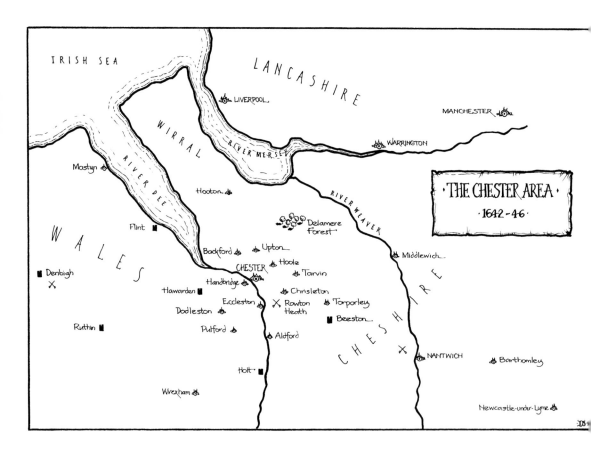

1. The Chester area, 1642–46.

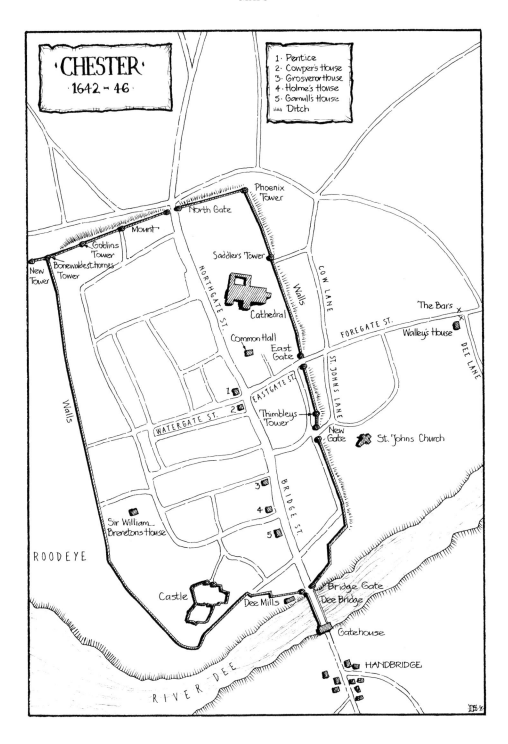

2. Chester, 1642–46.

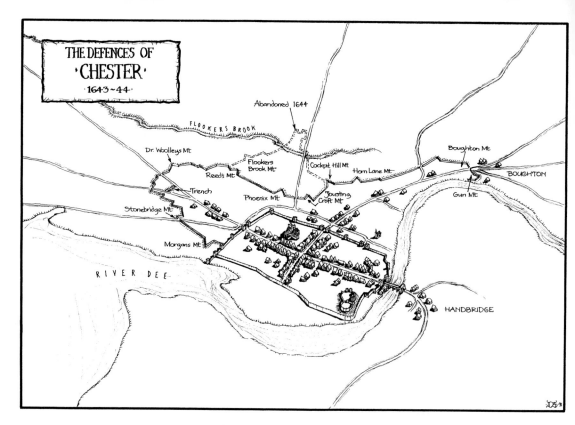

3. The Defences of Chester, 1643–44.

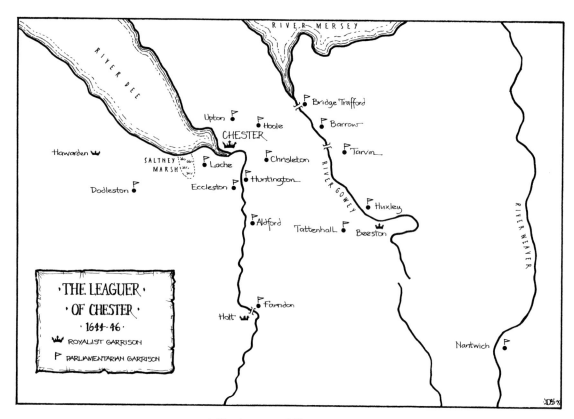

4. The Leaguer of Chester, 1644–46.

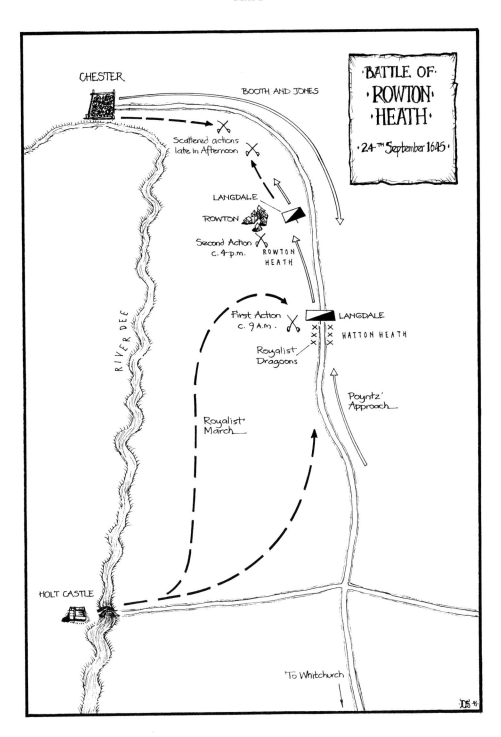

5. Battle of Rowton Heath.

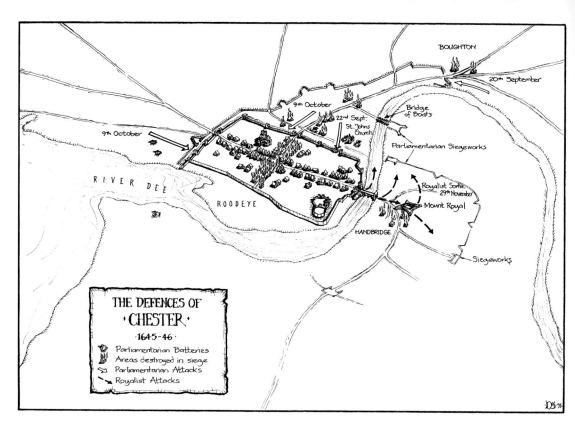

6. The Defences of Chester, 1645–46.

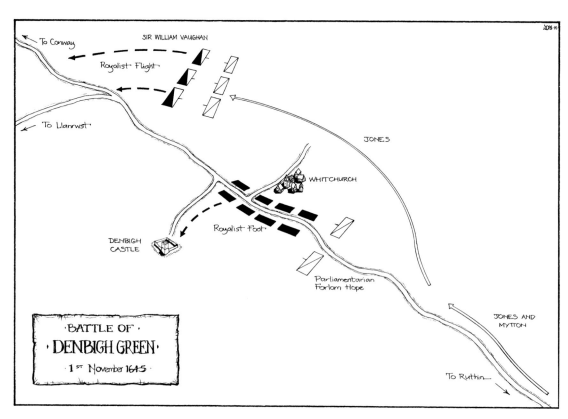

7. Battle of Denbigh Green.

NOTES

Abbreviations:

A.O.   Assembly Orders

JCAS   Journal of the Chester Archaeological Society

THSLC   Transactions of the Historic Society of Lancashire and Cheshire

TLCAS   Transactions of the Lancashire and Cheshire Antiquarian Society

CHAPTER 1 – 'MOST ANCIENTE CITIE'

1. R.N. Dore, 'The Dee and Mersey in the Civil War', in *THSLC*, vol. 136, 1986, pp.2–3; D.M. Woodward, 'The Overseas Trade of Chester, 1600–1650', in *THSLC*, vol. 122, 1970. For the troops bound for Ireland see R.H. Morris and P.H. Lawson, 'The Siege of Chester', in *JCAS*, 1923, pp.22–3; George Ormerod, *History of the County Palatine and City of Chester*, 2nd edn, 1882, vol. I, pp.237–8.

2. Dore, *op. cit.*

3. Annette M. Kennett (ed.), *Loyal Chester*, 1984, pp.9–10.

4. Annette M. Kennett (ed.), 'Galleries Which they Call the Rows', in *JCAS*, vol. 67, 1984.

5. Ormerod, *op. cit.*

6. Kennett, *Loyal Chester*, p.11.

7. P.W. Cullen and R. Hordern, *The Castles of Cheshire*, 1986, p.26.

8. Kennett, *op. cit*, p.11; D.M. Woodward, 'The Chester Leather Industry', in *THSLC*, vol. 119, 1968, pp.65–111.

9. A.M. Johnson, 'Politics in Chester during the Civil Wars and the Interregnum, 1640–62', in P. Clark and P. Slack (eds), *Crisis and Order in English Towns, 1500–1700*, 1972; see also Ronald Hutton, *The Royalist War Effort, 1642–1646*, 1982, pp.24–6.

10. J.P. Earwaker, 'The Four Randle Holmes of Chester, Antiquaries, Heralds and Genealogists, *c.*1571–1700', in *JCAS*, new series, vol. 41, 1892, pp.113–70.

11. R.N. Dore, 'The Early Life of Sir William Brereton, the Parliamentary Commander', in *TLCAS*, vol. 63, 1952–53, pp.1–26.

12. Eliot Wright, *op. cit.*; Keith Roberts, *Soldiers of the English Civil War: (1) Infantry*, Oxford, 1990; Keith Roberts, *Matchlock Musketeer, 1588–1688*, 2002.

13. Roberts, *Armies of the English Civil War*, *op. cit.*

14. *Ibid.*

CHAPTER 2 – WAR COMES TO CHESTER

1. Chester Assembly *Order Book* II, 512–518.

2. A.O. 325.

3. A.O. 465.

4. A.O. 527.

5. Randle Holme *Account* B.L. *Harleian MS* 2155 (reprinted Morris and Lawson, *op. cit.* p.215).

6. A.O. 555.

7. Morris and Lawson, pp.25–31; Hutton, *op. cit.*

8. A.O. 565.

9. John Barratt, *For Chester and King Charles: Gamull's Regiment of Foot*, 1993.

10. A.O. 567, 567a.

11. A.O. 568.

12. Hutton, pp.44–6.

13. Peter Newman, *Royalist Officers in England and Wales, 1642–1660: a Biographical Dictionary*, 1981, item 479.

14. The best complete survey is in Simon Ward, *Excavations at Chester: the Civil War Siegeworks*, 1987, pp.4–6. See also F. Simpson, *The Walls of Chester*, 1910, and T.J. Strickland, 'The North Wall', in *JCAS*, new series, vol. 65, 1982, pp.25–26.

15. Holme, *op. cit.*, pp.216–7.

16. Thomas Cowper, *Account of the Siege of Chester* (Cheshire County Record Office, DCC26).

17. Christopher Duffy, *Siege Warfare: the Fortress in the Early Modern World 1494–1660* 1979, p.157; Ward, *op. cit.*, pp.6–8.

18. Newman, *op. cit.*, item 231.

19. Quoted in Morris and Lawson, p.39.

20. A.O. 576.

21. Quoted in Morris and Lawson, p.39.

22. Mayor's *Letter Book* (CRO).

23. A.O. 586.

24. Hutton, p.65.

25. Holme, *op. cit.*

26. Parish Records of St Mary on the Hill, Chester, transcribed in Morris and Lawson, p.246.

27. Holme, *op. cit.*

28. *Ibid.*

29. A.O. 594, 601.

CHAPTER 3 – 'THE TYMES' TROUBLESOMENESSE'

1. A.O. 594; Morris and Lawson, p.44.

2. See John Lowe, 'The Campaign of the Irish-Royalist Army in Cheshire, November 1643–January 1644', in *THSLC*, vol. 111, 1959, pp.47–79.

3. H.M.C. *Portland MSS.* I, p.151.

4. Morris and Lawson, p.47.

5. B.L. *Harleian MS* 2155. f.126.

6. Chester Record Office *Letter Book (ML)*, f.21.

7. Bodleian Library, *Carte MS* 7, f.192.

8. Hutton, *op. cit.*, p.123.

9. *Dictionary of National Biography*; R.N. Dore (ed.), *Letter Books of Sir William Brereton*, Lancashire and Cheshire Record Society, vol. 128, 1990, p.586; Peter Young, *Marston Moor 1644*, 1970, pp.75–6.

10. *Harleian MS* 2125, f.135.

11. *Letter Book*; A.O. 599.

12. For the Nantwich campaign see John Barratt, *The Battle of Nantwich 1644*, 1993.

13. For an examination of this controversial episode see John Barratt, *Cavaliers: the Royalist Army at War 1642–1646*, 2000, pp.193–4.

14. British Library *Add.MS.* 18981, f.8.

15. Barratt, *Nantwich*, pp.12–20.

16. B.L. *Harleian MS* 2135, ff.40–3, 54–8.

17. B.L. *Harleian MS* 2125, f.320.

18. Eliot Warburton, *Memoirs of Prince Rupert and the Cavaliers*, 1849, I, p.494.

19. Chester City Record Office, *Letter Book*, f.24.

20. B.L. *Add. MS*, 18981, f.53.

21. Warburton, II, pp.375–6.

22. B.L. *Harleian MS*, f.320; Holme, p.220–1.

23. Ward, *Siegeworks*, p.11.

24. Holme, p.221.

25. John Barratt, *The Battle for York: Marston Moor 1644*, 2002, pp.49–52.

26. *Dictionary of National Biography.*

27. B.L. *Harleian MS* 2135, f.22.

28. *Ibid.* f.31.

29. *Ibid.* f.62.

30. Quoted Morris and Lawson, pp.62–3.

31. *Ibid.*, p.64.

32. For operations in Lancashire and Cheshire in July–August 1644, see Barratt, *Siege of Liverpool, op. cit.*

33. Andrew Abram, *The Battle of Montgomery 1644*, Bristol, 1994.

34. Barratt, *Siege of Liverpool*, p.21.

35. B.L. *Harleian MS* 2125, f.318.

CHAPTER 4 – THE LEAGUER BEGINS

1. A.O. 625, 629.

2. Stuart Reid, *Officers and Regiments of the Royalist Army*, n.d., *passim.*

3. Quoted John Lewis (ed.), *Your Most Humble and Most Obliged Servant*, 1995, pp.13–4.

4. See R.N. Dore (ed.), *Letter Books of Sir William Brereton*, vol. I, *Record Society of Lancashire and Cheshire*, vol. 123, 1983–84, item 241, note 1.

5. Thomas Carte, *Collection of Letters…* 1739, vol. 1, p.67.

6. Quoted in Morris and Lawson, p.68.

7. *Dictionary of National Biography.*

8. Dore, *op. cit.*, item 91, note 2.

9. *Ibid.*, item 385, note 1.

10. Nathaniel Lancaster, *A More exact Relation of Chester's Enlargement…*, 1646, p.18.

11. Quoted Morris and Lawson, p.70.

12. For Chrisleton see Holme, pp.221–3; Morris and Lawson, pp.70–72; Lancaster, p.19.

13. John, Lord Byron, *Account of the Siege of Chester* (Bod. Lib. *Rawlinson MS* B210) in

Cheshire Sheaf. 4th series, 6, 1971, p.4.

14. Quoted Morris and Lawson, p.72.

15. N.L.W. *Clennau Letters*, 544.

16. See Norman Tucker, *Royalist Major General Sir John Owen*, 1963, pp.34–41.

17. A.O. 636, 637.

18. Holme, p.222.

19. Morris and Lawson, pp.75–6.

20. Dore, *op. cit.*, item 16.

21. *Ibid.*, item 142.

22. *Ibid.*, item 125.

23. Bod. Lib. *Firth MS* C7 f.338.

24. Holme, p.223.

25. Dore, item 207.

26. *Ibid.*, item 221.

27. *Ibid.*, item 308.

28. Quoted Morris and Lawson, pp.78–9.

29. Dore, item 458.

30. *Ibid.*, item 509.

31. *Ibid.*, item 565.

32. Quoted Morris and Lawson, p.103.

CHAPTER 5 – CHESTER SURPRISED

1. Byron, *op. cit.*, pp.5–6.

2. *Ibid.*, p.6.

3. Ward, *Siegeworks*, p.11.

4. Byron, p.6.

5. Lancaster, *op.cit.*, p.21.

6. Byron, p.6.

7. *Ibid.*, p.7.

8. *Ibid.*

9. Lancaster, p.22.

10. *Ibid.*, pp.22–3.

11. *Ibid.*; Byron, p.7; Holme, *op. cit.*, p.223.

12. Quoted Morris and Lawson, *op. cit.*, p.108.

13. *Ibid.*

14. Byron, p.8.

15. Holme, p.224.

16. Byron, p.8.

17. Holme, *op. cit.*
18. *Ibid.*
19. *Ibid.*
20. Byron, p.8.
21. *Ibid.*
22. *Ibid.*; Holme, *op. cit*; Ward, pp.5, 28–30.
23. Holme, p.225.
24. Byron, p.8.
25. Holme, p.228.
26. Lancaster, pp.23–4.

CHAPTER 6 – THE BATTLE OF ROWTON HEATH

1. The campaign and battle are discussed in John Barratt, *The Siege of Chester and the Battle of Rowton Heath 1645*, 1994.
2. D. Parsons (ed.) *Diary of Sir Henry Slingsby*, 1838, p.98.
3. Lord Digby, *Account* in Thomas Carte, *Letters…*, 1739, vol. I, p.98.
4. Lancaster, *op. cit.*, p.24.
5. Byron, *op. cit.*, p.8.
6. Lancaster, p.24.
7. *Ibid.*
8. Colonel Parsons, *Relation*, quoted Morris and Lawson, *op. cit.*, p.118.
9. Lancaster, *op. cit.*
10. Parsons, *op. cit.*
11. Quoted Morris and Lawson, p.117.
12. *Ibid.*
13. *True Relation…* quoted Morris and Lawson, p.114.
14. *Ibid.*
15. Byron, *op. cit.*
16. Digby, *op. cit.*
17. Byron, *op. cit.*
18. *True Relation…* quoted Morris and Lawson, p.119.
19. Parsons, quoted Morris and Lawson, p.119.
20. *Ibid.*
21. *Ibid.*
22. Digby, *op. cit.*
23. Lancaster, *op. cit.*
24. *TrueRelation… op. cit.*
25. Lancaster, p.25.
26. *True Relation… op. cit.*
27. Quoted Morris and Lawson, p.119
28. Lists may be found in R.N. Dore (ed.), *Letter Books of Sir William Brereton*, vol. II, *Record Society of Lancashire and Cheshire*, 128, 1990, items 665, 666.

CHAPTER 7 – THE GREAT ASSAULT

1. Byron, *op. cit.*, p.11.
2. *Ibid.*
3. *Ibid.* Nicholas, Comte de St Pol was probably a professional soldier from Lorraine, who arrived in England by 1644, serving with the Royalists at Marston Moor. Byron seems to indicate some doubt as to the validity of St Pol's title. Henry Waite was a professional soldier who had served in Europe and with the Northern Royalists (Newman, *op. cit.*, items 1251, 1505).
4. *Ibid.*, pp.11–12.
5. *Ibid.*, p.11.
6. Quoted Morris and Lawson, p.123.
7. *Ibid.*, pp.123–4.
8. *Ibid.*, p.124.
9. *Ibid.*
10. Holme, pp.226–7.
11. *Ibid.*, p.227.
12. Byron, pp.12–13.
13. Lancaster, *op. cit.*, p.25.
14. Holme, p.227.
15. Byron, p.13.
16. Quoted Morris and Lawson, p.109.
17. Byron, p.13.
18. *Ibid.*, pp.13–14.

19. *Ibid.*, p.14.

20. *Ibid.*

21. *Ibid.*

22. See Lancaster, pp.25–6; Holme, pp.227–8; Byron, p.14. The new breach was about 15 yards west of the Goblin Tower, but owing to extensive later repair work is now difficult to identify precisely. (Ward, *op. cit.*, p.12).

23. Byron, p.14.

24. Holme, p.228.

25. Byron, pp.14–15.

26. Holme, p.228.

27. Byron, p.15.

28. Holme, p.229.

29. Letter of 14 October from Sir John Gell to the speaker (quoted Morris and Lawson, pp.129–30).

30. Byron, p.15.

31. Morris and Lawson, p.130.

32. Holme, p.228.

33. Byron, p.15.

CHAPTER 8 – TIGHTENING SIEGE

1. Byron, *op. cit.*, pp.15–16.

2. Ormonde managed to ship limited quantities of powder over to Byron, probably landing it initially in North Wales, on several occasions in 1644–45. (Bod. Lib. *Carte MS* 15, ff.671, 696; 16, f.256).

3. Byron, p.16.

4. Holme, *op. cit.*, p.229; Dore, *Letter Books…* II, *op. cit.*, Item 286.

5. Dore, Item 680.

6. *Ibid.*, Item 681.

7. *Ibid.*, Item 682.

8. *Ibid.*, Item 684.

9. *Ibid.*, Item 694.

10. Ward, *Siegeworks*, pp.12–13, 33–37.

11. Lancaster, *op. cit.*, p.28.

12. *Ibid.*

13. Holme, p.229.

14. *Ibid.*, p.230.

15. *Ibid.*

16. Ward, pp.30–32.

17. Byron, p.16.

18. Dore, Item 725.

19. *Ibid.*, Item 780.

20. Holme, p.230.

21. Byron, p.16.

22. Dore, Item 772.

23. *Ibid.*, item 791

24. For the action see Norman Tucker, *North Wales in the Civil War*, pp.82–88.

25. Dore, Item 806.

26. Holme, p.231.

27. Lancaster, p.28.

28. Holme, p.231.

29. *Ibid.*

30. *Ibid.*

31. Byron, p.17.

32. Dore, Item 830.

33. *Ibid.*, Item 840.

34. Ward, pp.12–13.

35. Dore, Item 840.

36. *Ibid.*, Item 832.

CHAPTER 9 – 'FIRE, FAMINE AND SWORD'

1. Stephen Bull, *Granadoe!*

2. Holme, *op. cit.*, p.231–2.

3. *Ibid.*

4. Byron, *op. cit.*, p.17.

5. Lancaster, *op. cit.*, p.29.

6. Dore, *op. cit.*, Item 875.

7. Byron, p.18.

8. Dore, Item 879.

9. Byron, pp.18–19.

10. *Ibid.*

11. Quoted Morris and Lawson, *op. cit.*, p.143.

12. *Ibid.*

13. H.M.C. *Portland MS I*, p.317.

14. Holme, pp.232–3.

15. Quoted Morris and Lawson, pp.146–7.

16. Holme, p.233.

17. Dore, Item 905.

18. Quoted Morris and Lawson, p.149.

19. Lancaster, p.30; Holme, p.234.

20. Holme, pp.234–5.

21. Dore, Item 978.

22. *Ibid.*, Item 997.

23. Byron, p.19.

24. Dore, Item 1042.

25. *Ibid.*, Item 1032.

26. *Ibid.*, Item 1033.

27. Holme, p.235.

28. Quoted Morris and Lawson, pp.150–1.

29. Dore, Item 1071.

30. *Ibid.*, Item 1081.

31. Holme, p.235.

32. Byron, p.19.

CHAPTER 10 – SURRENDER

1. Quoted Morris and Lawson, *op. cit.*, pp.189–90.

2. Dore, *op. cit.*, Item 1177.

3. *Ibid.*, Item 1184.

4. *Ibid.*, Item 1198.

5. Quoted Morris and Lawson, p.173.

6. Byron, *op. cit.*, p.20.

7. Dore, Item 1249.

8. *Ibid.*, Item 1203.

9. Quoted Morris and Lawson, p.173.

10. Byron, p.20.

11. Dore, Item 1249.

12. Byron, p.20.

13. Quoted Morris and Lawson, p.238.

14. Byron, p.21.

15. Morris and Lawson, pp.238–243.

16. *Cowper MS* C.C.R. DCC.

17. Byron, p.21.

18. *Ibid.*

19. *Ibid.*

20. *Ibid.*

21. *Ibid.*

22. Dore, Item 1251.

23. *Ibid.*, Item 1253.

24. Byron, p.20.

25. Lancaster, p.6.

26. *Ibid.*

27. Quoted Morris and Lawson, p.179.

28. Lancaster, p.30.

29. Quoted Morris and Lawson, p.183.

30. *Ibid.*, p.190.

31. Byron, p.20.

32. Quoted Morris and Lawson, p.186.

33. *Ibid.*, p.187.

34. *Ibid.*, p.188.

35. *Ibid.*, p.191.

36. Quoted Morris and Lawson, pp.192–5.

37. Byron, p.21.

CHAPTER 11 – AFTERMATH

1. See Norman Tucker, *op. cit.* pp.117–128.

2. H.M.C. *Portland MS* I, p.352.

3. Quoted Morris and Lawson, *op. cit.*, pp.203–5.

4. *Ibid.*, pp.206–9.

5. *Ibid.*, p.210; Kennett, *Loyal Chester*, p.28.

6. Morris and Lawson, pp.206–7.

APPENDIX – A TOUR OF CIVIL WAR CHESTER

1. Of the many guidebooks to Chester, perhaps the most useful in this connection is Brian Harris, *Chester*, 1979. Simon Ward's book on the fortifications is also invaluable.

BIBLIOGRAPHY

PRIMARY SOURCES

Bodleian Library: *Carte MS 7*.

British Library: *Additional MS 18981*; *Harleian MSS 2155* (Randle Holme 'Journal'), *2125*, *2135*.

Byron, Lord John, *Account of the Siege of Chester* (Bodleian Libray, Rawlinson MS B210), reprinted in *Cheshire Sheaf*, 4th series, 6, 1971.

Calendar of State Papers, Domestic Series, 1641–47, London, 1887.

Carte, Thomas, *Collection of Original Letters and Papers...* London, 1739.

Cheshire County Record Office: *Account of the Siege of Chester* (by Thomas Cowper), 1764, D.C.C. 26.

Chester City Record Office: *Assembly Order Book (A.O.); Mayor's Letter Book (M.L.); Assembly Files (A.F.); Mayor's Files (M.F.)*.

Dore, R.N. (ed.), *Letter Books of Sir William Brereton, Record Society of Lancashire and Cheshire*, vols 123 (1983–4), 128, (1990).

Historical Manuscripts Commission, *Thirteenth Report*, London, 1891.

Lewis, John (ed.), *The Siege of Chester: Nathaniel Lancaster's Narrative*, Nottingham, 1987.

Lewis, John (ed.), *Your Most Humble and Most Obliged Servant: Ten Secluded Letters from the Lord Byron*, Newtown, 1995.

Malbon, Thomas, *Memorials of the Civil War in Cheshire, Record Society of Lancashire and Cheshire*, vol.19, 1889.

Warburton, Eliot (ed.), *Memoirs of Prince Rupert and the Cavaliers*, 3 vols, London, 1849.

SECONDARY WORKS

Barratt, John, *The Battle for York: Marston Moor 1644*, Stroud, 2002.

Barratt, John, *The Battle of Rowton Heath and the Siege of Chester*, Bristol, 1994.

Barratt, John, *Cavaliers: the Royalist Army at War, 1642–46*, Stroud, 2000.

Barratt, John, *Civil War Stronghold: Beeston Castle at War, 1642–45*, Birkenhead, 1993.

Barratt, John, *For Chester and King Charles: Sir Francis Gamull's Regiment and the Defence of Chester*, Birkenhead, 1995.

Barratt, John, *The Nantwich Campaign, 1644*, Birkenhead, 1995.

Barratt, John, *The Siege of Liverpool and the Lancashire Campaign, 1644*, Bristol, 1994.

Blackmore, David, *Arms and Armour of the English Civil Wars*, London, 1990.

Bull, Stephen, *Granadoe!* Southend-on-Sea, 1990.

Dore, R.N., 'The Cheshire Rising of 1659', in *TLCAS*, vol. 69, 1959.

Dore, R. N., *The Civil War in Cheshire*, Chester, 1966.

Dore, R.N., 'Dee and Mersey in the Civil War', in *THSLC*, vol. 136. 1986.

Dore, R.N., 'The Early Life of Sir William Brereton, the Parliamentary Commander', in *TLCAS*, vol. 63, 1952–53.

Dore, R.N., 'Sir Thomas Myddleton's Attempted Conquest of Powys, 1644–5', in *Montgomeryshire Collections*, vol. 57, 1962.

Dore, R.N., 'Sir William Brereton's Siege of Chester and the Campaign of Naseby', in *TLCAS*, vol. 67, 1957.

Duffy, Christopher, *Siege Warfare: the Fortress in the Early Modern World, 1494–1660*, London, 1979.

Earwaker, J.P., 'The Four Randle Holmes of Chester, Antiquarians, Heralds and Genealogists, *c.*1571–1707', in *JCAS*, ns. Vol. 41, 1892.

Edwards, Peter, *Dealing in Death: The Arms Trade and the British Civil Wars, 1638–52*, Stroud, 2000.

Eliott-Wright, Philipp, *English Civil War*, London, 1997.

Geddes, William, 'The Chester Mint', in *THSLC*, vol. 107, 1955.

Harris, Brian, *Chester*, Edinburgh, 1979.

Hemingway, J., *History of the City of Chester*, Chester, 1838.

Hutton, Ronald, *The Royalist War Effort, 1642–46*, London, 1982.

Johnson, A.M., *Politics in Chester During the Civil Wars and Interregnum 1640–62*, in P. Clark and P. Slack (eds), *Crisis and Order in English Towns, 1500–1700*, London, 1972.

Kennett, Annette M. (ed.), *Loyal Chester*, Chester 1984.

Lowe, John, 'Campaign of the Irish-Royalist Army in Cheshire, November 1643–January 1644', in *THSLC*, vol. 111, 1959.

Lowe, John and Dore, R.N., 'The Battle of Nantwich 25 January 1644' in *THSLC*, vol. 113. 1961.

Morrill, John, *Cheshire 1630–1660*, Oxford, 1974.

Morris, Rupert H, and Lawson, Phillip H., *The Siege of Chester, 1643–1646*, Chester, 1923.

Newman, Peter, *Biographical Dictionary of Royalist Officers in England and Wales*, New York, 1981.

Ormerod, George, *History of the County Palatine and City of Chester*, London, 1882.

Phillips, John Rowland, *Memoirs of the Civil War in Wales and the Marches*, 2 vols, London, 1874.

Porter, Stephen, *Destruction in the English Civil Wars*, Stroud, 1994.

Reid, Stuart, *Officers and Regiments of the Royalist Army*, Southend-on-Sea, n.d.

Roberts, Keith, *Matchlock Musketeer: English Infantry, 1588–1689*, Oxford, 2002.

Roberts, Keith, *Soldiers of the ECW: 1. Infantry*, Oxford, 1989.

Ryder, Ian, *An English Army for Ireland*, Southend-on-Sea, 1987.

Simpson, F., *The Walls of Chester*, Chester 1910.

Strickland, T.J., 'The North Wall', in *JCAS*, ns, vol. 65, 1982.

Tincey, John, *Ironsides: English Cavalry, 1588–1689*, Oxford, 2002.

Tincey, John, *Soldiers of the ECW: 2. Cavalry*, Oxford, 1990.

Tucker, Norman, *Denbighshire Officers in the Civil War*, Colwyn Bay, n.d.

Tucker, Norman, *North Wales in the Civil War*, Denbigh, 1958.

Tucker, Norman, *Royalist Major-General: Sir John Owen*, Colwyn Bay, 1959.

Tucker, Norman, *Royalist Officers of North Wales 1642–1660*, Denbigh, 1961.

Ward, Simon, *Excavations at Chester: the Civil War Siegeworks, 1642–46*, Chester, 1987.

Woodward, D.M., 'The Overseas Trade of Chester, 1600–1650', in *THSLC*, vol. 122, 1970.

INDEX

Numerals in *italics* refer to illustrations